Y0-BSM-732

OTHER BOOKS BY BOB WEINSTEIN

Résumés Don't Get Jobs: The Realities and Myths of Job Hunting

"I'll Work for Free"

Jobs for the 21st Century

How to Switch Careers

How to Get a Job in Hard Times

"So What if I'm 50?"

WHO SAYS THERE ARE NO JOBS OUT THERE?

25 IRREVERENT RULES FOR GETTING A JOB

Bob Weinstein

McGRAW-HILL
New York San Francisco Washington, D.C. Auckland Bogotá
Caracas Lisbon London Madrid Mexico City Milan
Montreal New Delhi San Juan Singapore
Sydney Tokyo Toronto

Library of Congress Cataloging-in-Publication Data

Weinstein, Bob.
Who says there are no jobs out there? : 25 irreverent rules for getting a job / Bob Weinstein.
p. cm.
Includes index.
ISBN 0-07-069209-2 (pbk.)
1. Job hunting. I. Title.
HF5382.7.W445 1997
650.14—dc20 96-33055
CIP

McGraw-Hill

A Division of The ***McGraw-Hill*** *Companies*

1 2 3 4 5 6 7 8 9 0 DOC/DOC 9 0 1 0 9 8 7 6

ISBN 0-07-069209-2

The sponsoring editor for this book was Betsy Brown, the editing supervisor was Jane Palmieri, the designer was Michael Mendelsohn, and the production supervisor was Donald Schmidt. It was set in Sabon by Priscilla Beer of McGraw-Hill's Professional Publishing Group composition unit.

Printed and bound by R. R. Donnelley & Sons Company.

This book is printed on recycled, acid-free paper containing a minimum of 50% recycled, de-inked fiber.

For Bonnie, Jenny, Josh, and Enrique

CONTENTS

INTRODUCTION

YOU'RE ON YOUR OWN! WELCOME TO A BRAVE NEW WORLD

It seems like just yesterday that conquering the job market was a logical process. You could manipulate it. Employers, especially Fortune 500 companies, the sprawling bulwarks of American industry, made promises and kept them. Following World War II, the country settled back to enjoy a surreal existence. For almost 40 years, America enjoyed extended prosperity as a new work ethic flourished. Corporations rewarded loyalty and hard work with lifetime employment. Millions of Americans lived storybook lives, devoting entire careers to their organizations. The corporation became a surrogate parent, meeting workers' most basic needs. It guaranteed a career and offered training, not to mention footing all or part of their offspring's college tuition. Company towns cropped up where each family's new generation grew up knowing a job awaited them.

The company was a veritable Rock of Gibraltar, an indestructible support beam in workers' lives. If a worker was in financial straits, loans were provided at low interest rates. When disbelievers questioned the corporate lifestyle, the loyal rebutted, "Don't be cynical. The *company* will take care of you." For a while, it did just that.

Workers seldom considered that these amorphous legal entities were run by fallible men and women. By the time they digested that sobering reality, it was too late. That once proud bastion of power was beginning to crumble. America had lost its competitive edge as

Japan sprinted to the lead, emerging as the technological trendsetter. Japan, Pacific Rim countries, and even many western European countries were making better products more cheaply. American industry was in trouble.

The death knell sounded and heads rolled throughout corporate America. Household-name companies we all trusted, the icons of American capitalism, began laying off loyal workers and exiling millions to early retirement. Corporate fortresses the likes of IBM, Eastman Kodak, TRW, Xerox, American Express, Digital Equipment Corporation, Amoco, and R. H. Macy handed out pink slips en masse. And they haven't stopped yet.

The winds of change swept through America like a tornado, leaving untold destruction and confusion in its path. No one was prepared. Unlike in the past, the layoffs were permanent. Even if the company recouped losses or underwent restructuring, few workers were rehired.

Loyal employees' hard work was repaid with a perfunctory handshake and a severance package. If lucky, you walked away with maybe a couple of months of outplacement counseling. In short, you were forced to start over.

And what a blow it was. The baby boomer generation was confused. That's not the way it was supposed to be. The deal went bad. The American dream turned into a nightmare. Corporations broke their promise. Just 30 years ago, futurists and economists predicted a 4-day workweek, retirement at 62, comfortable pensions, and (how can we forget?) the cushion of social security. You remember social security, the idealistic product of the New Deal administration? It was an incredible concept, but not any longer. If you're banking on social security benefits when you're too feeble to work any longer, you're in for a rude awakening. Social security benefits will no longer be able to meet most of our retirement needs. The disarming trust is that the Social Security Administration is running out of money. In 1984, approximately half the benefits were taxable; a decade later, the tax rate jumped to more than 85 percent. Like they say, the more you make, the more the government takes. According to the Social Security Administration, in 1945 there were approximately 42 workers for every beneficiary. By 1950, the number had dropped to 16.5; by 1994, it tumbled to 3.2; and by the year 2010, it's projected at 2.9 workers for every beneficiary.

Numbers don't lie. With people living longer (older Americans are projected to outnumber teenagers 2 to 1 by the year 2025), the number of retirees eligible for social security will continue to grow, but the worker base needed to support them will not keep pace. So much for New Deal idealism.

Welcome to the new job game. It brings new rules with a new game plan. All you have to do is learn to master the rules and secure jobs.

For many, change is hard to digest. It's human nature to hold on to the status quo. A lot of people are wailing the blues and crying, "Things will never be the same again." That's an easy cop-out. It's true, things will never be the same again. And that's good. If they were, we wouldn't change, get better, or move forward. That spells atrophy and stagnation in anyone's language.

Look critically at the past half-century and you'll see it was not the utopia it appears to be. How great could it be when millions blindly put all their faith in a corporation? How good are things if you abdicate responsibility for your fate to others? With no control over our fate or destiny, we're living only marginally. It's kind of like self-imposed slavery. Ultimately, you pay the hefty price if you're suddenly thrown out into the cold to fend for yourself. What's more, you're cut off from the real world in this womblike atmosphere. You only think it's warm and secure. The truth is you're not growing and changing. You are stuck. And that's not what life should be about. It ought to be an adventure and an exciting one at that. Along the way, you should hit peaks, valleys, and some bumpy roads that test your endurance and survival skills.

Let's move on. Look at the past as a chapter in your life. You're turning a page to a new part where incredible opportunities and experiences await you—if you pursue them.

You've heard it before: Change is healthy. Learning how to fend for yourself under new conditions is challenging, not to mention fun. You face a bold and exciting job market. Master it and you stand to reap more satisfying rewards than your predecessors. Unlike prior job markets, it's more demanding and competitive, yet the psychological and physical payoffs are bigger. Digest the information packed in these chapters and you'll get a leg up on your competition.

Unlike the past, there are no guarantees or certainties. Employers are making no promises. They're not saying, "We're one big family," "You've got a home with us," or "We take care of our own." If they are being honest, it will be more like, "Do a great job and we'll see." In short, you're a human machine. If an employer can find a better, faster, or cheaper model, you will be history. Cruel, vicious, and heartless, you say. Not at all. It's called "reality," equaling smart business. If you had poured your sweat and money into getting a company off the ground, how would you feel? Sleepless nights are spent agonizing over competition banging at your door. Would you dare hire anyone who isn't ready to sweat blood? You can't argue with that kind of straight-up logic. It's just plain common sense.

Thanks to a global marketplace and America's recouping its position as an industrial leader, we've seen a return of a frontier mentality and 1990s-style rugged individualism. It's kill or be killed. Companies have seen the light. The days of stockpiling people are over. No more free rides. If you can't make money for an employer, you're out. Prove yourself indispensable and you stand a chance of conquering a corner office and all the trappings accompanying it. If you've got what it takes, you can go to the top far faster than your counterparts of a decade ago.

Corporate America deserves this book. It's high time to shatter the myth of the corporate Valhalla once and for all. I'm going to show you how to thrive in the new corporate jungle.

Job security, guarantees, yearly raises, and pensions are out the window. If you're going to make it, you'll do it with initiative, creativity, hard work, street smarts, resilience, and unshakable self-confidence. The only one who is going to take care of you is *you*.

Are you ready to conquer the new job market? Stick with me and

I'll show you how by passing on proven job-hunting strategies. These are techniques successful job hunters use. Many are offbeat, unconventional tactics you won't find in traditional career books. But take it from me, they work. I know. I've used them all.

Yes, it's a tough job market. But don't for a nanosecond believe anyone who tells you there are no jobs. There are plenty if you know where to look.

Let's start by debunking the myth of finding the perfect job. Sorry, it doesn't exist any more—in fact, it never did.

Bob Weinstein

ACKNOWLEDGMENTS

I've written a lot of career books, but this one was the most fun. I couldn't have done it without help from a gifted battalion of researchers and supporters that include my friend and colleague Tom Popp for helping me build a perfect manuscript; my kids Jenny and Josh for cheering me over the finish line; my son-in-law Enrique "Titti" Ball for tirelessly clipping articles from *The Boston Globe* and looting libraries and magazine stands across the United States; my wife Bonnie for putting up with a demented journalist; my Mom for giving birth to a gifted writer; my Dad for giving me the cynical mind of a philosopher; and last but not least, my drinking buddies—T. Pete Bonner, Bob Forbes, Bobby Chait, Eddie Brodsky, and Salvatore "Sally Boy" D'Nunzio.

CHAPTER 1

WHADDAYA MEAN GET A REAL JOB?

RULE 1 Forget about getting a real job. Concentrate instead on work needing to be done.

You're probably screaming, "Why did I buy this dumb book if I can't get a real job?" If you think you've been taken to the cleaners, you're wrong. The point is "real jobs," the mythical goal in the 1940s, 1950s, 1960s, and 1970s, are gone forever.

Back in the 1960s when I graduated college, my buddies and I talked about getting "real jobs." What better example than the legendary scene in the film *The Graduate* (1966), when a fresh-out-of-college Dustin Hoffman was told by his future father-in-law to "get into plastics." The older man was convinced he was imparting the secret of the universe. Back then, it was good advice. The emerging plastics industry represented a fertile hothouse of "real jobs."

A real job was the real thing. It was *the* job, a serious job, as opposed to the string of summer, part-time, and odd jobs I had held since high school. A real job was a "professional white collar" job. It was clean and stable and, most important, it offered a future. It was a long-term job commitment. It conjured images of respectability and settling down. It was a home away from home. Your boss was a surrogate parent. In short, a real job spelled CAREER in billboard-sized letters. It also meant working for a big company, the bigger the better. You were headed for the fast track if you conquered a job at one of the bastions of American capitalism—IBM, DuPont, Ford, GM, and other companies of that ilk.

The earlier you could latch onto a real job, the better off you would be. The superstars who had the good sense to put out job feelers before they graduated often walked straight out of school into a secure job with a promising future. These were the folks we envied.

Capturing the real job was every college grad's fantasy. Some scored immediately; others waited months, even a year or two to conquer the right one. If you lucked out, your real job turned into a perfect job. That meant a lifetime position with everything—perks, benefits, advancement potential, bonuses, you name it. This is the job that takes care of not only you but your whole family. It will pay for your kids' education and give them jobs when they graduate. This is the kind of job my relatives held. Maybe yours did too. Needless to say, they advised me to follow in their footsteps.

The message was loud and clear. Get yourself one of these jobs and you're made. Your future is secure. And, if you are an aggressive hell-raiser, there is no reason you can't leapfrog up the corporate ladder and hold a top job—maybe even the number-one spot. Hey, someone's got to do it. You reason, "Why couldn't it be me?"

You get the picture. That was job hunting back then. My generation was raised thinking you ought to hold one, maybe two, jobs your entire life. That's what working and career building were all about. Spending 15 to 20 years with one company was par for the course. Today, that's inconceivable. It worked for the baby-boomer generation until the balloon burst in the 1970s. At that time, American industry suddenly pulled a wild card from the deck and began dumping loyal perfect workers with machinelike efficiency. So much for lifetime security. The party ended, the band stopped playing, the house suddenly faded to black. Americans had to sober up fast. When thousands of companies dumped millions of workers, we knew the 40-year period of post-World War II security was indeed a statistical footnote, a historical blip. The "organization man" was put on a life-support system and fading quickly. It was just a matter of time before we pulled the plug.

Things will never be the same. And that's good, because it's not only healthier but more exciting this way. Take the hint and think like a fatalist or a philosopher. Maybe we weren't meant to hold one job. Living is all about tasting, experimenting, and working at different jobs and careers. Stay with me. We'll get into career changing and job hopping later on.

Conventional Job Goes the Way of the Dinosaur

Once you've digested the fact that perfect and real jobs are throwbacks to another era, I've got another zinger for you: The conventional notion of a job has been blown to smithereens. I'm not the first one to say it either. William Bridges, author of *Job Shift,* insists that the traditional job has gone the way of dinosaurs, the Edsel, and black-and-white television. He's put the job on the endangered species list. Organizations are becoming what Bridges calls "dejobbed." That means they're getting work done without hiring full-timers for conventional jobs. It's easily accomplished by hiring "temps" (provided by temporary service firms), using contract/project workers, and leasing employees.

It sounds radical, but Bridges proves it is logical. Prior to the Industrial Revolution, there was no such thing as a job per se, with someone reporting to work and doing the same task 8 hours a day, 5 days a week. Explains Bridges: "People worked on a shifting cluster of tasks in a variety of locations on a schedule set by the sun, the weather, and the needs of the day." Things changed at the turn of the nineteenth century when, as a newly industrialized nation took shape, work was packaged and the job emerged.

Then, the concept of a job made good sense. It was a way to get a great deal of work done in a short time. It was a simple concept that paid off for employees and employers. Yet it was a flawed social artifact destined for a brief life. It was too neat, not to mention unreal. The present situation proves it.

CHAPTER ONE

Welcome to the Future

As you are discovering, illusions and fantasies about the past are fast being crushed. All it takes is a few months of searching for work to discover this firsthand. In the 1970s, futurists predicted a high-speed electronic society that resembled something out of a Buck Rogers episode. Today, it's reality. Within the next few years, nomadic workers will be working out of cars, at airports, and at shifting workplaces. All the equipment you need to run a multimillion corporation—cellular phone, pocket computer, and portable fax—can be crammed into an attaché case.

Like the migrant workers of the late 1930s, job searchers will be moving around the country looking for exciting career opportunities. They'll go where the action is as work becomes less departmentalized.

Job searchers will be constantly on the move, following the action. Despite all our sophisticated technology, we've come full circle. We're not very different from the early craftspeople who fashioned their own work styles. Like them, we must be creative chameleons—adaptable, flexible, multifaceted, open-minded learning sponges capable of packing our bags on a moment's notice and heading off in new directions searching for fertile opportunities.

Bridges was on the money when he said smart workers must forget about jobs completely and concentrate on "work needing to be done." I urge you to heed this precious advice.

Let's start by learning how to reinvent ourselves.

CHAPTER 2

YOU'RE A NICE PERSON. BIG DEAL! BUT ARE YOU A HIGH-FUNCTIONING CYBORG?

Companies want products, not people.

So you are a great person. You are reliable, hardworking, honest, and trustworthy, a compassionate family person who loves God, country, parenthood, and the Big Mac. And you're a compulsive recycler to boot. Fantastic! Does that mean you ought to conquer jobs faster than anyone else? Not on your life. Getting a job is not like passing into heaven.

You're wasting your time trying to be perfect. Employers aren't looking for saints, they're looking for *products*, durable human machines who can work like cyborgs—and do perfect work to boot. Unreasonable, you shout. Well, welcome to the global marketplace.

You had better learn to think of yourself as a product, better yet, an exquisitely wrapped one, if you hope to land a job faster than your competition.

Employers care about one thing: getting the job done perfectly. The human part of the equation comes later—if at all. Yes, there's a chance you and your boss may hit it off and play racquetball during lunch and swig boilermakers after work. But don't count on it. In fact, you are better off keeping it strictly professional. It makes for a cleaner and sharper relationship and avoids any confusion about your roles.

Too often, friendship between employer and employee creates problems. Topping the list is unrealistic expectations on the employee's part. Spend enough time with the boss, and you begin to expect favors, special treatment, maybe even promotions before you're ready. Then unexpectedly, all hell breaks loose and your expectations are blown to bits. Whatever the reason, the business is in trouble. It has lost market share, sales have plummeted, or a major client or customer has jumped ship for a competitor. The solution? Recent hires must be given their walking papers. You happen to be among the last batch employed. Suddenly, your bubble bursts when you're given 2 weeks' notice to clear your desk and turn in your keys. "Sorry, Margaret, it's nothing personal. You're a hell of a worker, a great person, and you play a mean game of racquetball. But hey, this is business and, as much as it hurts, it has to come before friendship. But count on me for a great reference. Good luck—and keep in touch."

In the span of a 12-minute conversation, your friendly boss suddenly transforms into a monster replete with horns and claws. He's no longer your sports and drinking buddy, but your employer. One minute you have the world locked up, the next you're agonizing about paying next month's rent and meeting your car and student loan payments.

Afterward, after thinking long and hard about the upsetting event, you realize your boss had no choice. Let's face it, you'd do the same thing if it was your company. It doesn't mean employers and employees can't ever be friends. They can, if they understand the dynamics of the relationship. The most important dynamic is seeing the respective roles clearly. All goes well when both parts of the work equation (employer and employee) fulfill their obligations. Your role is to do a hell of a job and never break down. The company's role is to stay healthy and grow. Once either side falters—you screw up or the company encounters rough seas—the game plan changes and it's time to slip on your flak jacket, because change is in the air. Accept these realities and you are well on your way to successfully wheeling and dealing in this crazy new job market. The obvious benefit is developing razor-sharp objectivity concerning your career prospects.

ADVICE

Sell yourself as a high-functioning product rather than as a feeling, fallible human being. That's a fundamental commandment of this new job market. Remember: Profits are more important than people. It's easy to say, yet hard to understand. The best way to start is by totally reevaluating yourself.

Workaholic Warriors Wanted. Sell Benefits! "I Don't Care about Your Qualifications, Just Tell Me What You Can Do for Me!"

So what if you graduated at the top of your class? You're smarter than Einstein and are listed in the *Guinness Book of Records* with an IQ of 900. Does all that mean you're going to win a job faster than anyone else? Sorry! All it means is you're supersmart and did well in school. I hate to knock icons and the $100,000 you blew on a fancy college education at a blue-chip school. But the truth is your incredible academic past doesn't hold the same weight it once would have. They should have confronted you with that reality when you were killing yourself to earn good grades.

Back in the 1950s and 1960s, employers, especially glitzy Fortune 500 companies, went out of their way to hire brainiacs, top-of-class students who had potential. They especially liked to hire specialists, people who could do one thing exceptionally well. They paid them fabulous salaries with great benefits and perks—maybe tossed a snazzy company car in the package—and then threw these employees in cubicles and told them to do their thing 8 hours a day. That's what they were paid to do. It was a neat, clean, and simple arrangement. No wonder presidents of midsize and large companies had little idea of who worked for them. The well-paid specialists were afraid to come out of their cubicles. The obvious advantage for management, however, was that it took some of the pain out of firing these smart people. They weren't real living and breathing human beings—just job titles, functions, and payroll numbers.

That was then. These days, companies, especially large ones, don't think too much of specialists. They've been replaced by high-powered generalists, jack-of-all-trades mavericks who do everything well. They're veritable work machines, ready to roll up their sleeves and exhaust all means to get the job done. These folks are not relegated to tiny cubicles where they won't be heard or seen. Management wants workers to be "out there," visible, vocal, and independent thinkers. Uppermost, they've got to be superproductive.

In a severe market with competitors breathing down their necks, employers don't have time to invest weeks interviewing job candidates. Most know exactly what they want. They demand candidates who can cut right to the chase and sell their assets to the hilt. They don't want candidates who are skittish about tooting their own horns. When it comes to fattening the proverbial bottom line, modesty doesn't fly. Being humble about broadcasting your talents only points up your naiveté.

The folks who capture jobs fast waste no time tying their skills into the bottom-line results. They don't need a start-up or training period. Their engines are racing and waiting for the signal to bolt out from behind the starting line. Quick studies, they're up to speed in a couple of days. Even if a task is not humanly possible, they can convince employers otherwise. If nothing else, they capture points for aggressive and feisty attitudes alone.

Don't be uptight about following suit. Solve a pressing problem during your first meeting with an employer and you've batted a home run clear out of the ballpark. "If you don't mind my offering a suggestion, Mr. Attlebrain, you'd do better testing sales reps in a new region for 6 months to see if the location has potential. Once you see results, slowly phase out the reps and put in your own people. You will have more control and you'll see bigger returns."

The employer scratches his head, sighs, takes a deep breath, and says, "You know, you've got something. I never thought of that, nor has anyone else at the company. I like the way you think." That heartfelt comment translates to a rave review, putting you miles ahead of your competition.

The message: Sell *benefits, benefits, benefits*—and don't stop. The more you drive them home, the faster employers believe it.

Flip the Relationship
Understand Both Sides of the Equation

A megamistake made by job searchers is not fully grasping what employers want. The two big questions you ought to be asking yourself are:

1. What the heck is the company looking for?
2. If I were running this company, what kind of job applicant would I hire?

These obvious questions are seldom asked. Job candidates expend a lot of energy researching the company and talking to anyone who knows anything, yet most fail to have a precise understanding of employers' needs. Once that is accomplished, you can put yourself in the employer's shoes. Trust me, it puts a whole other spin on the situation. Suddenly, the job in question becomes crystal clear. It goes from black and white to technicolor, and images change from two- to three-dimensional. The job is no longer an abstraction; it becomes real. The best part is it's more attainable than before. The folks securing jobs quickly and automatically perform this exercise. Once they are eyeball-to-eyeball with employers, they're able to lunge for the jugular and relentlessly sell their talents until the employer gives them a job just to get rid of them.

Having a solid idea about what employers want helps you make a good impression.

"I'm Not Looking for a Handout or a Permanent Home" Roll Up Your Sleeves and Meet a Temporary Need

Even though you think you can meet an employer's needs, don't plan on doing so permanently. That's archaic thinking. Remember what I said about real and perfect jobs in the preceding chapter.

Concentrate on meeting a temporary need. If anything more comes of it, you'll have lucked out. Statistics say you'll spend 2 to 5 years at a job and then move on to a better or different one—if you're not booted out beforehand. Yes, there's a chance you'll stumble on the job of jobs, bolt to the top, and be there for the next half-century. But don't mortgage your house on it or you'll be living on the street.

Remember, you're a human machine, disposable and recyclable. It means you must get ready to work yourself into a coronary, if that's what it takes. No joke. If you ask a potential employer what the working hours are, I guarantee you won't get the job. The employer will conclude, "This little lady is a clock watcher, a nine-to-fiver. Clearly not for us." Employers want to know that your job *is* your life. They don't want to know about the 12 kids you have in day care or the sickly mother you've been supporting since you were 11 years old. They don't want to hear any Dickensian tales. *They don't care.*

No, you're not getting paid to work around the clock and relinquish family and friends for your job. But don't ever confront an employer with that obvious reality.

The sobering truth is Americans are working harder than ever. In fact, we're the hardest-working people on the planet. The U.S. Bureau of Labor Statistics reports that 22.8 percent of the nation's 87.4 million full-time workers spend 49 or more hours a week on the job. A decade ago, only 17.7 percent worked that hard.

For some compelling statistics, check out *The Overworked American: The Unexpected Decline of Leisure* by Juliet Schor, an associate professor of economics at Harvard University. Schor debunks the myth of the 4-day workweek that has been projected by economists since the 1950s. Economists were convinced that economic progress would lead to a better lifestyle and early retirement for most Americans. The last decade proved they are wrong. A significant number of workers, especially the survivors of downsizings fortunate enough to find jobs, are working into their mid-seventies and beyond. And many Americans are working 14- and 16-hour workdays just to pay their bills. Schor says that translates to 60 to 90 minutes less sleep a night.

But don't get upset about any of this. The truth is hard work is good for you. Yes, it's fun to play, but believe me you'd get pretty sick of playing golf, growing tomatoes and zucchini, and seeing the world. People are meant to be productive and creative. That spells work. I've got more to say about the benefits of work in my final chapter about retirement.

"I'm Taking Care of Number 1, Thank You" Your First Allegiance Is to Yourself

Think of yourself as a survivor in a perilous battlefield. It requires a me-against-the-world attitude. It only sounds selfish and egocentric. Soon you'll see it's a smart and mature strategy leading to success.

If you learned anything from this erratic job market, it is that no one is going to take care of you. That doesn't mean you should come across as a loner, a cynical drifter ambling down the highway of life.

The "I'm taking care of number one" philosophy is only an attitude, the equivalent of mental C-rations keeping you alive in the tough job market terrain. That attitude implies having the flexibility to do whatever is necessary to play the game successfully.

Keep in mind that employers still want team players, folks who can work together "stimulating and maximizing everyone's special skills," as the human resources robots put it. If it makes you feel better, call it the "group" or "organizational" model. Even if you're a card-carrying misanthrope who hated camp, school, your entire family, and even Ronald McDonald, never stop convincing employers you're a "people person." They love hearing this boast.

The fact is you're not going anywhere if you don't nurture and cultivate relationships. So, overcome any people hang-ups you have to accomplish your immediate goal: getting a job. If you've got a problem with people, get thee to a shrink pronto. And keep it to yourself. More on building lasting, productive relationships in the networking chapter ahead.

Attitude Is Everything

When you boil down all of the above, you are left with a critical job-hunting tenet: Employers are looking for special people willing to give blood. This attitude drives them home.

Attitude is a tough word to define. It's in your eyes, body language, and speech patterns. It's the way you shake hands, answer questions, and volunteer information. Books like Napoleon Hill's *Think and Grow Rich* and Walter Germaine's *The Magic Power of Your Mind* are all about cultivating positive attitudes. Warner Erhard, the founder of EST, rocketed to millionaire status creating a whole new language around building a positive attitude. What did it matter if most of the language had been said before. Supersalesman that he was, Erhard convinced thousands he was the second coming.

Most people don't have the foggiest idea how to build a good attitude, so they turn to charismatic hucksters who could sell ice in the Antarctic for answers. For a price, these gurus give the inside word to them in spades, complete with language, rules, and codes of behavior.

But when you boil down all the buzzwords and strip away the fanfare, you discover that the nucleus of a great attitude consists of optimism, hope, persistence, and the unquenchable drive to succeed and do something well. That's what a great attitude is all about, and that's precisely what employers want to see. Believe me, if you're doing what you love and you're hell-bent on being the very best, transmitting that kind of optimism is easy. Those who get to the top make two very critical assumptions early in the game: First, they realize they have a lot to learn. Second, they know they are going to experience plenty of resistance and failure along the way. Thomas Edison is a classic example. When he was inventing the electric light, he failed 1200 times before he finally got it to work. When a journalist asked him how he dealt with 1200 failures, Edison replied, "I did not fail 1200 times. I was successful in finding 1200 ways the light bulb didn't work." How's that for a great attitude?

Let's move on and find out how to market ourselves to the hilt.

CHAPTER 3

"BUY ME—PLEASE!" COLOR ME MARKET READY

RULE 3 Package yourself 1990s-style.

I bet your teachers told you that everything in life is complicated. And that it takes a college degree and a formula résumé to get a job. Safe and secure behind the ivy-covered world of academia, what do teachers know anyway? Street smarts is precisely what most academics lack—and what's needed to get a job in this crazy market. Combine street smarts with basic marketing principles and you've got a foolproof job-snaring strategy. It doesn't take a business degree to understand this, just plain common sense.

The essentials of smart job getting can be reduced to four timeless marketing commandments.

1. *Identify buyers.* When reading a book, you begin on the first page and end on the last. Logical, right? Job hunting is similar. As simplistic as that seems, many job hunters are like whirling dervishes going nowhere. They're expending a lot of energy but accomplishing little. They're trying to do a million things at once yet accomplishing nothing. If you do that long enough, you'll exhaust yourself, not to mention be chronically unemployed. Don't get upset if I hit a familiar chord. It goes part and parcel with the human condition.

The job-hunting process starts with identifying buyers, the potential companies that may hire you. Decide whom you want to work for. A large, midsize, or small company? Be flexible, because there are no absolutes in this market.

Most job hunters have definite ideas about the size and type of organization for which they think they'd like to work. But it's dangerous to limit your options. Conditions are very different than they were in the past.

A decade ago, most large companies were unwieldy organizational behemoths, bogged down by layers of middle-management inefficiency and dead weight. Decision making was snail-like and frustrating. I'm not saying all large companies have streamlined their acts. As a result of the restructuring of American industry that began in the mid-1970s, many corporate executives overhauled their organizations. Beyond paring ranks, they've eliminated layers and simplified the decision-making process. Many of the international conglomerates have carved themselves into autonomous, self-governing businesses. They're functioning more like midsize and small organizations than like large companies. More change is in the works. Aside from structural changes, big companies are searching for new blood to march them into the millennium.

But don't let myths and bad experiences stop you from pursuing large companies. The same goes for midsize firms. Many of the once conservative middle-management companies have loosened their belts, opening their doors to anyone with the talent, initiative, and guts to move them forward. Don't for a moment think these changes mean organizations are reverting to a New Age version of 1960s corporate paternalism. It's more basic. They simply realize they're not going to grow and prosper without smart people. They had to get knocked down a few times to come to an obvious conclusion: *Give talented people the proper tools and they'll achieve incredible feats.* Progress and growth are not about sticking with tried-and-true routines; instead they're about testing new ideas and taking chances.

Apply that same thinking to small companies. The U.S. Small Business Administration (SBA) defines a small company as one with fewer than 500 employees or sales under $10 million. That's pretty broad, not to mention confusing. According to that definition, plenty of small companies are actually quite substantial. Still, you'd be better off assuming your average small company has fewer than 20 employees and sales under $5 million.

The exciting news is that thanks to corporate upheaval, small business ranks are expanding every year. Tired of long periods of unemployment and bouncing from one company to another, corporate refugees are testing the entrepreneurial surf. While most will perish within 3 years of start-up, many of these companies stand an excellent chance of becoming big players.

Investigate the small company arena. Forget the tiny mom-and-pop businesses and pursue the young thoroughbreds, the entrepreneurial start-ups bearing seeds of greatness. These are the buyers to target, the companies hungry for bright people anxious to roll up their sleeves and prove themselves. It's not just a great concept that's starting these companies along the fast lane; it's the entrepreneurial compulsion to rocket them to greatness.

You don't have to go far to find household-name companies that were once brash young upstarts singled out for greatness. Not too long ago Microsoft, Sun Microsystems, and Nike were tiny companies nobody took seriously. Today they're superstars, entrepreneurial legends

REMEMBER: No one starts out big. Some companies are fortunate to fly out of the gate with big funding, but most start with little or no money. Either way, as with any company, they must learn to walk before they can run. As any entrepreneur will tell you, making it to adolescence is just one of many gauntlets a new business must get through.

Finding buyers is not difficult. Start by plugging yourself into fertile information sources to uncover leads. Start with the obvious places and then get creative. Read daily papers religiously—want ads to business news—7 days a week. Plug into the trade press so you're on top of every newsletter covering your industry. Make sure you're on your professional or trade association's mailing list to receive its newsletters, press releases, and briefings on upcoming meetings. Become an information junkie. You just never know when you're going to uncover a gold mine lead.

Finally, become a relentless networker so you attract information from an endless number of sources. Networking can be a big bonus, but sadly, is often done poorly. We'll get into the fine points of networking later when I pass on incredible secrets.

ADVICE

Avoid narrow-minded, rigid thinking so you can objectively look at all kinds of potential buyers. Be open-minded when it comes to evaluating corporate cultures as well. Even historically stodgy, conservative companies are spinning on their heels and swerving into the fast lane.

And don't say you'd never consider relocating. Sure, relocating is a gigantic step. It means leaving family and friends, maybe uprooting kids from school, and abandoning a comfortable lifestyle to start over. It's a radical move. Yet it also could signal a once-in-a-lifetime career opportunity, not to mention a better, more enriching life. Remember, this is the 1990s. We're living in a global society, home of the "new nomads," as futurist Alvin Toffler described it in his classic *Future Shock*, published in the 1970s. Toffler predicted a mobile society in which Americans were constantly moving in search of new opportunities. Thanks to technology, the world is now a seemingly smaller place. We can work anywhere. At the rate we're going, it won't be long before companies are opening divisions on other planets. Sound far-out? It wasn't too long ago that people laughed at the mere mention of breaking the sound barrier. Now it's old hat. And wheeling-and-dealing in cyberspace used to be the fodder of sci-fi writers. Now companies and job seekers are surfing the Internet in search of opportunities. Never say never.

2. *Don't try to be all things to all employers.* Pretend you own a company that just created a snazzy new widget. It's faster and cheaper, lasts longer, and does the job better than anything out there. Terrific? How are you going to get folks to buy it? Are you going to market it to everyone or identify a tight market that has bought widgets in the past and is likely to endorse a new product? If you picked the latter strategy, you're thinking like a marketing professional. Marketing mavens stress the importance of strategically positioning product. Try to sell the wrong product to the wrong market and you're destined to foul out. *Examples:* Xerox and RCA lost billions when they tried to sell computers. Or imagine Kentucky Fried Chicken trying to peddle quiche to loyal customers.

   Apply this critical principle to yourself. After you've identified buyers, go to the next step and find out if they need you. It sounds pretty obvious, right? Wrong! Millions of job hunters invest time and money sending unsolicited résumés to companies. (An unsolicited résumé is one sent blindly hoping it will find a buyer.) Does anyone actually think Fortune 500 or midsized companies or stressed-out entrepreneurs running small companies are going to schedule an interview if there are no jobs? It's estimated that Fortune 500 companies get as many as 1 million unsolicited résumés a year. It doesn't take much imagination to figure out what happens to 99 percent of them. They're trashed, most of them unread. I'll address the dangers of using résumés later. For now, think about the silliness of the buckshot approach of mistakenly waiting for a company to pull your résumé out of a stack of 500 and say, "Hey, I can't believe it. This is just the guy we've been looking for." Only in your dreams will that happen.

What's more, most unsolicited résumés are addressed to titles rather than real people. How would you feel if you were the manager of a department and you got a cover letter and résumé addressed to your title? I bet you'd say, "Is she kidding? First, I don't need anyone in my department, and if I did, you'd think she'd go to the trouble to find out my name. It only takes a phone call." Managers are not wrong in thinking that way.

Point made. *Buckshot approaches don't work.* If you hope to snare a job, you'd better fire up the gray matter and start thinking like a pro. Get with the program. You cannot create a need when there is none. And don't be naive enough to think that a random hit-or-miss strategy will work. It's like playing the lottery. If you enjoy gambling on impossible odds, I guarantee you'll be unemployed for the rest of your life.

The folks getting jobs quickly are targeting themselves at the applicable employers. They're doing so in three ways. The first and easiest is simply uncovering a real job lead, either through a want ad or the grapevine.

The second is uncovering an emerging job not yet fully developed and advertised. *Examples:* A start-up company is gearing up for product launch or an established company has reorganized or expanded and is weeks or months away from beefing up its staff. It happens every day. If you're a voracious reader with a discerning eye you'll spot such companies. For example, while perusing the business pages of your local paper, you're drawn like a magnet to a tiny story on the last page that reads, "Paddywoddy Cookies gears up to launch snack division." To your delight, you discover the company has invested more than $5 million to get the division off the ground. It goes on to explain the kinds of products and what incredible competition the company faces. What the article doesn't say is Paddywoddy will soon be hiring people to run it. That's your signal to drop everything and pursue that lead with a vengeance.

The third, and most difficult, method of selective targeting is going after potential employers that are not actively recruiting people. Sounds nuts, doesn't it? It is if you firmly believe employers always know what they need and cannot be sold on hiring a hot prospect. Now we're talking about raising the game to a whole new level. Using such a sophisticated targeting strategy requires Sherlock Holmes-like smarts. It starts by making two astute assumptions about employers. First, they don't have their acts together all the time, and second, they can be sold on new ideas.

We've all bought into the myth that employers know what they're looking for. That's what my family told me. The boss is smart—omniscient—and unfailingly makes great decisions. Shut up, don't make waves, do what you are told, and collect your paycheck. I don't have to tell you what that kind of thinking has done to a couple of generations of job searchers.

Putting fantasies and myths aside, no company head, especially one running a small or midsize company, is totally in control. Unlike in large companies, where decision making is more often done by consensus, in small and midsize companies managers are obsessing about every nitty-gritty detail. They're worried about competition breathing down their necks, bringing new product to market, paying bills, and getting employees to give 100 percent. No matter how hard-nosed they seem, all employers are open to good ideas that will improve business. They can be sold on anyone who can fatten the company's bottom line. Open yourself up to this fact of business life and you'll start seeing opportunities requiring sophisticated targeted marketing. It means applying your strengths and talents to companies that potentially need new employees.

TRUE STORY: A 32-year-old recently laid-off computer programmer was looking for a job the old-fashioned way until he saw an opportunity no one else had thought of. He read about a large regional office supply store that had expanded into selling computers and accessories. Rather than apply for a job as a computer salesperson, he sent the president a business proposal. To promote the sale of computers, he suggested offering a two-pronged service aimed at home buyers and businesspeople. For home buyers, the store staff would select the appropriate software and teach customers how to use it; for businesspeople, a consulting service would teach customers how to use technology to maximize efficiency. The idea was to take the work and fear out of buying and using computers, plus trigger additional sales through a technical consulting service. What's more, the programmer had the good sense to suggest a 6- to 8-week trial period. If it didn't work, he'd walk, no hard feelings. In short, he was making the employer an offer he couldn't refuse. The happy conclusion? He got the job. What's more, he's still there. The idea was so successful, this enterprising programmer now heads a three-person computer service department.

Talk about positioning yourself. The above job searcher did it brilliantly. He created not only a job for himself, but a brand-new profit center for the company. That's a win-win situation for everyone.

3. *Get there first.* Did you ever think about why you pick certain products as you amble down supermarket aisles? Why is it you unconsciously pick one brand over another to toss into your shopping basket? Why buy Coca-Cola instead of one of the dozens of generic brands? The reason is you think Coca-Cola is the best because it was the first popular cola on the market. Is it really the best? Absolutely not. But that doesn't matter. What matters is you think it's the best. Similarly, despite what's happened to IBM over the past few years, many people still swear it makes the best computers. The truth is there are some 50 competitors offering comparable, often better, products, at better prices.

   The big point is we associate "first" with "best." Marketing gurus Al Ries and Jack Trout, authors of marketing classics *Positioning, Marketing Warfare,* and *Bottom-Up Marketing* (McGraw-Hill) pull down hefty consulting fees telling companies how to be "first."

Apply that critical marketing tenet to your job hunt. Realistically speaking, you can't always be first, but you can give it your best shot. The sobering reality is if you don't get there first, someone else will. More important is thinking competitively and thinking of the job hunt as a race. The runner who bounds over the finish line first gets the prize, the best job. At that victorious moment, you will have competed like a seasoned pro.

4. *Be the best.* Right alongside the concept of being first is the notion of quality, another hot area which has spawned a profitable consulting niche for management heavies. You don't need to read Peter Drucker or Tom Peters to know what quality is all about. Plain and simple, a good product is a quality product. If it's something we use, like a car, bike, washing machine, or lawn mower, we use words like *durable, sturdy, high-performing, safe,* and *affordable* to describe it. In the food category, the essence of quality gets muddied by personal preferences. Kentucky Fried Chicken, Kellogg's Corn Flakes, and Haagen Dazs ice cream have withstood the test of time because they're excellent products. Health-food fanatics think otherwise, yet millions of consumers swear by them.

   There is no such thing as a perfect product, yet those that have lasted have improved and changed with the times. That goes for the marketing, the packaging, and the products themselves. Their manufacturers worked hard at making them the best in their category.

   You ought to take a similar approach in readying yourself for the job hunt. Like a battleship being outfitted for war, make sure you are ready to overtake the enemy, your competition.

   Two major components are necessary to be the best. First is physically preparing yourself. That includes everything from investigating potential companies you'd like to work for and networking to looking your best. Second, and equally important, is actually thinking and believing you're the best. High-paid headhunters insist a candidate's eyes unfailingly telegraph that all-important trait. The eyes of a high-powered candidate sparkle, transmitting confidence, self-assurance, openness, a willingness to try anything or meet anyone.

Think about it. What do your eyes reveal about you? If you've got low self-confidence, this is the time to work on it. It doesn't mean you need a shrink. It may be as basic as taking control of your job search. The more control you have over all aspects of the job hunt, the more confident you'll be. Remember how you felt in school when you walked into an exam knowing you would ace it? You were prepared, a veritable encyclopedia of information. Your eyes radiated confidence and strength. On the other hand, if you pulled an all-nighter hoping you'd squeak by with a passing grade, your eyes would appear downcast. You hadn't even looked at the exam and you felt beaten. Keep that analogy in mind when preparing to take your job-hunting act on the road.

Mark Twain said, "A man cannot be comfortable without his own approval." Amen.

Thoughts about Smart Selling
Avoid the Hard Sell

Now that you've digested these four marketing commandments, some thoughts about selling yourself. Salespeople have gotten mixed reviews over the last century. On the negative side, images of loser salesmen like Willie Loman in Arthur Miller's *Death of a Salesman* come to mind, or the con artists in Barry Levinson's timeless classic film *Tin Men,* about aluminum-siding salesmen in Baltimore.

Once you get beyond the negative stereotypes of salespeople as drummers, hucksters, fast talkers, and hustlers who can charm you into buying anything from snake oil to vacuum cleaners, you'll discover that everyone must master the selling basics in order to succeed. Plain and simple, if you hope to land a job selling a product or service, you'd better know how to sell yourself first.

Whether the idea of selling excites or disgusts you, a simple fact of life is we're all selling something. Scholars, writers, and painters must also find and build the right connections to sell their wares. The selling process, however, is the same as selling hamburgers.

Fact: Buyers are not going to find you. You must find and entice them to buy you and your skills.

Marketing and sales skills are blood relatives. You can't have one without the other. Whereas marketing is the process of getting a product or service to the buyer, selling is convincing someone to buy it. In your case, this means getting someone to hire you.

We'll get into selling tactics in detail when we talk about interview strategies. Prior to that critical pass-or-fail interview, you're going to be selling yourself to leads and contacts who hopefully will open doors for you. The trick is making a good impression every step of the way. The best way to do so is by avoiding the hard-sell tactics associated with cliché snake oil salespeople.

Hard sell is a turnoff. If you want proof, think of all the offensive phone calls you get from people pitching products and services you don't need. Telemarketing salespeople are the worst offenders. Not only do they have an uncanny knack for calling at the worst times, but they're relentless. Telemarketing salespeople peddling financial-planning services and penny stocks are notorious for this tactic. I'm sure you can think of plenty of offensive salespeople who have annoyed you with tasteless come-on tactics. Whether they're selling cars or computers, they're enraging rather than engaging you.

Lay It on the Line

Take the hint and play it straight. Avoid fancy footwork and smoke-and-mirrors tactics. Accept the fact that everyone you meet is busy and can't afford to waste a second. When you connect with a potentially hot lead, say what's on your mind in the clearest and simplest way, express your gratitude, and move on.

Likewise, learn how to read people. If you're getting negative vibes, take the hint and retreat gracefully. Think of all those nasty telemarketers who call as soon as you set foot in the door. They sense you're frayed and can't wait to get off the phone, yet they keep blabbering until you slam down the phone in disgust. You'd think they would get the message. Don't make the same mistake.

Remember, your competition is either right behind or a few steps ahead of you. Time is of the essence. Whatever you do, don't give up.

Now let's master some jungle job-snatching tactics.

CHAPTER 4

JUNGLE TACTICS GET JOBS

RULE 4 **Get yourself a flak jacket and hit the streets.**

Old assumptions and myths only slow you down. Forget everything you've been told about job hunting. There are no rules. It's every man and woman for themselves. Think of the job market as a battle zone in the midst of a heated jungle war. Win it and you conquer the prize—a great job with a super salary, incredible perks, and power to spare. Jungle tactics employing strategy, thought, shrewdness, and street smarts can help you win the war.

Imagine what evolutionist Charles Darwin would say if he delivered a seminar on job hunting. He'd probably say the job market is life in microcosm. Those who conquer jobs quickly have mastered the survival game. They're the best, brightest, toughest, and strongest. What's more, they'll go the furthest. They've mastered jungle tactics, the custom-made aggressive strategies needed to find the best jobs first.

A jungle tactic is an advanced preparatory tactic that gets you a job before your competition. Like special military forces doing reconnaissance work before the main army launches an invasion, you need to fashion invasion tactics that get you to the job beachhead first.

Jungle tacticians belong to an elite group of job hunters. They're single-minded, free-spirited mavericks who insist upon doing things their own way. They're contrarians. If everyone is following the crowd, they'll spin on their heels and go the other way.

Interested in enlisting in this elite group? The parameters are pretty loose. The best part is you have the freedom to do anything you want. That's right, just be your own person.

Start by trashing your copy of *What Color Is Your Parachute?*, Richard Bolles' perennial best-seller on job hunting. Everyone reading that outdated tome is doing the exact same thing. Bolles' advice could fly in the 1970s, but not in the free-spirited, no-rules 1990s. Job hunting by the numbers is a waste of time. So stop running around scheduling information interviews, getting in touch with yourself, rewriting your résumé, and following the crowd. That's the antithesis of jungle tactics. Start operating as a free agent, a job-hunting mercenary. Abandon all the standard protocols.

Jungle tactics are based upon recognizing your uniqueness and developing strategies that work only for you. Remember: *You're a bona fide original who refuses to be herded.* Don't try to fit into someone else's mold.

Sounds great, doesn't it? I've just lifted an enormous burden from your shoulders. Conforming can be exhausting, not to mention depressing, because it leaves no room for creativity and individual expression. The sooner you start doing things in your own style, the faster you'll get a job. Face it. Following the crowd is downright boring.

Contrary to what my colleagues have been saying for the past 20 years, job getting doesn't consist of established rules to be followed to the letter. On the contrary. It's about bending rules and making the system work for you.

To appreciate jungle tactics, let's start by blasting two well-entrenched job-hunting myths that have foiled job hunters.

- *College degrees yield jobs.* College degrees help and I wouldn't dare suggest building a career with only a high school diploma. If you can find a way to conquer a college degree, by all means try. Nevertheless, thousands of successful people have never stepped foot inside a college classroom.
- *Designing a career path is the surest way to be successful.* Maybe that was true a decade ago, but not any more. How

can anyone forge a career path without the foggiest idea of what the world will be like in the next year?

Just a short while ago, only one career path existed: the linear corporate track. You would start in the mailroom and work your way to a corner office. Countless books have been written about plotting the right track by hanging out with the right people, squeezing the grapevine, and positioning yourself in power jobs. These days, many more options abound. If you haven't noticed, not everyone is part of the traditional 9-to-5 paycheck culture, enjoying benefits, perks, and pensions. A growing number of people are working on a contract, project, or part-time basis. And millions have practically elevated temping to a lifestyle. More on that later. Put them all together and you've got the components of what the economists call the contingent work force, which is growing faster than the full-time work force. In 1970 approximately 16 percent of the population held multiple jobs, according to the U.S. Bureau of Labor Statistics. Last year that number jumped more than 44 percent.

Now that we've blown two job-hunting myths to smithereens, let's fashion jungle tactics that can help you hack your way through the job labyrinth like a high-paid mercenary.

Proven Jungle Principles

Here are three proven jungle principles leading to jobs.

1. *Getting a job is more difficult than keeping one.* As much as we bitch and moan about jobs we've endured and all the horrendous bosses who came with them, holding down a job isn't difficult. It requires little initiative or independent thinking. Just do what's expected and don't make waves. Get to work before your boss and don't leave before him (or her). After all, your days are laid out for you. Pretty basic stuff. If you're smart and aggressive, you'll move up the organizational ladder.

   Job hunting, however, requires a different set of skills. The toughest part is setting schedules and routines and keeping to them. It sounds simple, but ask job holders who endorse jungle tactics and they'll tell you it's not easy in the beginning. It's tough getting up in the morning when you have no routines structuring your day. Most of the day, you're going to be by yourself. No cronies to schmooze with whenever you feel like it. What's more, the rewards of job hunting are elusive. There's no telling what each day will bring. And then there are the horrendous unavoidable chores accompanying job hunting—reading nonstop, mailing letters, talking to countless people, researching companies for hours. Needless to say, much of this grunt work won't pay off. The ultimate trick is prioritizing all this stuff into a day.

Sounds horrible, doesn't it? What's more, you better get used to the job-hunting routines—better yet, learn to enjoy them. It's no wonder most job hunters give short shrift to the job-hunting process. After all, it requires energy, thought, and discipline. Here's how to do it.

- *Dive right in and immerse yourself in the process.* You've heard the expression "Getting a job is a job in itself." Well, it's true. Most people, however, don't turn the hunt into a full-time job because it's so easy whiling away entire days doing next to nothing. All you have to do is stay up late, watching old movies, wake up late, and commiserate with out-of-work job colleagues who prefer to blame others for their fate rather than do something about it. When all is said and done, it doesn't matter whether you were a victim of circumstance (politics, downsizing, consolidation, merger, bankruptcy) or you simply screwed up. The simple truth is you must get your act together and find another job.

  As soon as you join the ranks of the unemployed, you're commander-in-chief of a one-person army—yourself. Do you have the guts, fortitude, and street smarts to march to victory? The burden is on you.
- *Create routines and schedules and stick to them.* Many job

hunters don't get new positions quickly because they don't put in enough time. I can't give you the ultimate working schedule. What works for somebody else may not work for you. Everyone has different rhythms. The trick is finding your stride by experimenting with different schedules. For now, I'm only going to emphasize the importance of creating job-hunting routines. In Chapter 7, I've outlined a sample schedule to use as a guide for maximizing time.

I may sound like a drill sergeant, but the harder you are on yourself—the more hours and effort you put into job hunting—the faster you'll see results.

Success doesn't happen by itself. Don't wait for lucky breaks either. Create your own luck. Comedian and film director Woody Allen nailed it when he said 80 percent of success can be reduced to two words: *Show up!* Remember, the enemy (other job hunters) may be using their own jungle tactics and putting in long hours as well. What better motivation to work longer and smarter?

2. *Invest time in unconventional sleuth work.* The more sophisticated and creative you are in gathering and assessing information, the better your job game. Whoever gets the hottest tips first stands the best chance of scoring.

   Keep your information-gathering antennae up 24 hours a day. *Hot tip:* Get tomorrow's news today. Most large daily newspapers print their Sunday want-ad sections on either Thursday or Friday and deliver them to newsstands late Friday night or early Saturday. Here's an opportunity to beat your competition by responding to potential jobs a day earlier than everyone else. Check your mailbox pickup schedule. Many have one or two pickups on Saturday. If they don't, the main office surely does, which means your letter will wind up on an employer's desk by 10 a.m. Monday. Similarly, it pays to investigate other print outlets to find out how to get your hands on them before they hit the newsstands. All it takes is a few phone calls.

3. *Play hunches, act on dreams, listen to your inner voice.* Don't

knock intuition, premonition, or gut feeling. They all produce a strange feeling called a hunch. There's nothing scientific about them either. They're hard to describe because they're based on nothing more than an unsubstantiated feeling or inner voice. Yet you can't ignore them. If you're the least bit skeptical, read biographies of famous people who acted on their instincts or gut feelings. They weren't sure why they did certain things; all they knew was a powerful force propelled them to action. Most times, hunches don't pay off. Yet you never know when a sudden, mysterious feeling will yield surprising results. Dreams can also open doors if you interpret them. It doesn't take a Freudian scholar to appreciate their meaning. A dream is your subconscious begging to be heard. When you're spending 12 to 14 hours a day either working or thinking about your job search, chances are you're going to dream about it too. Some of these dreams will be eye-openers, pointing you to job leads.

If you want proof, check out the countless great inventions triggered by dreams. Isaac Singer, the inventor of the sewing machine, attributed the spark of the idea to a dream. Take the hint. If a dream opens a hidden channel, act on it immediately. Pull yourself out of bed and write it down. If you don't, it will evaporate as quickly as it surfaced. *Caution:* As with hunches and feelings, there are no guarantees dreams will pay off. But are you willing to pass up a potential opportunity?

The big message is keep all your senses open. Become an information sponge, soaking up tips and tidbits everywhere.

Jungle Tactics for Young and Older Job Searchers

Jungle tactics are for everyone, young and old. Consider the following:

Strategies for Teens

Jungle tactics are to be shared with your children. The younger, the better. A big mistake is waiting until your offspring reach college before explaining the job-hunting facts of life. The sooner you do it, the better they'll begin to understand the world of work, the supply-and-demand factors impacting it, and how we find and hold jobs. The best time to do so is during the adolescent and preteen years.

The faster your offspring learn job-hunting realities, the better prepared they'll be to compete in a high-speed world. The job market is only going to become more competitive. If you have to think like a military strategist to find a job, your children and their children will also. Back in the old days you could actually start looking for a job after you graduated from college. Not any more. Insightful college students lay the groundwork for a career during their freshman and sophomore years. They enroll in internship and cooperative education projects and pile up solid work experience so they can walk out of school and into great jobs.

The bad news is the job market will always be competitive. The good news is there are more options for breaking in at the entry level. Two proven avenues leading to jobs are internships and cooperative education programs.

Cooperative education and internship programs are not new. Co-op programs link academic curriculum with a series of paid jobs in a field related to a student's study or career goals. Internships are designed learning arrangements, lasting from 1 month to 2 years, in which objectives are set with established tasks and projects. The emphasis is on working to learn, not earn. Although internships can lead to employment, co-op students are in the best position to capture solid jobs. Depending on who you speak to, 45 to 70 percent of co-op students are offered full-time jobs with their co-op employers. Many employers predict that by the year 2000, the number of co-op programs will triple.

Working your way through college used to mean juggling a string of factory and menial office jobs around your class schedule. More often than not, no correlation existed between the type of work and the student's major or planned career. But not any more. In the 1990s, working your way through college will mean hooking up with a high-ranked co-op program. The beauty of a co-op program is it allows students to pay for a significant share of their tuition by working at a job (or jobs) related to their major. Students receive college credits for their work experience. One semester of full-time work usually equals three college credits.

Northeastern University in Boston, for example, boasts the largest co-op program in the country, with 8500 of its 10,500 day students enrolled in such arrangements. Its students earn about $80 million a year, defraying 75 percent of their tuition. But the best part is they get practical work experience, which often results in a job offer from their co-op employers. Equally important, it offers financial assistance to all students regardless of family income or other financial-aid criteria, without leaving students burdened with debts for several years after graduation.

Colleges offer two types of co-op arrangements: the traditional alternating plan and the more popular parallel arrangement. In the former, students work one semester and go to school the next, whereas in the latter, they combine work and study by going to school full-time while working part-time.

For a brochure and a roster of U.S. colleges offering programs, send $3 to the National Commission for Cooperative Education (NCCE), 360 Huntington Avenue, 384 CP, Boston, MA 02115. The Cooperative Education Association, 117710 Beltsville Drive, Suite 520, Beltsville, MD 20705, has a database of 800 co-op programs throughout the United States. Write to the association with your requirements—school type (public or private), size, location, and proposed major. They'll do a free search and tell you what's out there.

If co-op programs aren't available, there are probably plenty of internship opportunities. Ideally, internships integrate theory, practice, and constant reflection. In short, the emphasis is on working to learn, not earn, although many internships pay small stipends. The good news is internships are more popular than ever. A report from the College Placement Council, a career-planning information resource, finds that an increasing number of college recruiters are looking to fill open positions with student interns. In 1985, one out of seven undergraduates enrolled in internship programs. Today, more than one in five undergraduates jump at internship opportunities. They'd be foolish not to. A recommended source is the National Society for Experiential Education's National Directory of Internships, which is updated yearly. Request it by writing to 3509 Haworth Drive, Suite 207, Raleigh, NC 27609-7229.

Take the hint and tell your kids about these neat options. Not only will you make their lives easier, you'll be lightening the burden on yourself. Face it, if your progeny don't capture jobs when they graduate, I don't have to tell you where their temporary digs are going to be. If that isn't an impetus, I don't know what is.

Tactics for Older Job Searchers

My recently published "*So What If I'm 50?*" is an entire tome of job-hunting strategies for older workers. Sadly, this powerful group doesn't realize how much clout they have. The 50-plus generation will grow by 12 million in the 1990s. What's more, in this decade alone they're going to have more than $300 billion in spending power.

The problem is most 50-plus job hunters don't realize how many skills they offer. Thousands of companies would just about kill for workers who are experienced, mature, reliable, and quick studies. There is a growing army of older workers out there who fit the bill. Intimidated by a youth-obsessed culture that no longer venerates its elders, they don't realize they've got the marketing edge. If you fall into this resilient group, don't hang your head in shame. Harness your talents to get what you want.

But what do you do if you don't have the slightest idea of what career to pursue? Believe me, the world won't come to a shattering halt waiting for you to decide. All it takes is a little insight and hard work. Turn the page and I'll tell you how.

CHAPTER 5

CAREER CRISIS AHEAD! APPLY THE BRAKES "WHAT THE HECK AM I GOING TO DO WITH MY LIFE?"

All it takes to find a career passion is time, insight, and a sense of adventure.

Before we go any further, let's make a slight but important detour to address a critical issue: What do you do when you are not sure what kind of job you want? Don't worry. It doesn't mean you'll roam the streets for the rest of your life trying to find your true calling.

The fact is this happens more and more in this crazy job market. The reasons are twofold. First, constant economic and technological changes are forcing people to rethink their career objectives. Second, because of rampant change, employers are more accepting of career changers and willing to give them a chance.

It may be a tough job market, but it's also one which encourages experimentation. Employers are willing to accept creative mavericks changing career direction or searching for the mythical perfect job.

Three or four decades ago, the quest for meaningful, soul-enhancing work was virtually unheard of. If you're from immigrant stock, as I am, or are a product of the Depression, searching for a perfect job that nurtured soul and intellect and paid a great salary was not the objective. The goal was *snaring any job* that paid enough to support and feed your family. No other priorities existed. If you stumbled on something you actually loved doing, you lucked out. As soon as my ancestors stepped off the boat, they jumped on the first jobs they could find. Some thrived and achieved success; others settled and wallowed in mediocrity, never working to their potential for fear of tempting fate. The reality was they had few alternatives. They took what they could get.

The same goes for the Depression generation. If you watched your parents survive for months without finding a job, scrimping and cutting back on bare necessities, the value of work suddenly took on a whole new meaning. A job became a coveted and precious goal. As with the millions of people who streamed into this country to escape poverty, a job, any job, translated to prosperity. It's no wonder these immigrants made plenty of compromises. They had no choice. Their attitude was don't get fancy, take chances, or do anything crazy, or else you'll find yourself sleeping in an alley starving to death.

Thankfully, times have changed. The economy has improved. Sweatshops have, for the most part, disappeared and so have other vile forms of exploitative employment. More jobs are available in flexible working arrangements. Uppermost, change is built into all aspects of the job picture. And facing a career crisis is just one of them. Unlike my humble-stock ancestors from "the old country," today's generation can afford the luxury of experimentation until they find their true calling.

THE BOTTOM LINE: Career crisis is nothing to be ashamed of. It's a product of the times. It's particularly evident at two critical career points: among entry-level workers and among seasoned workers who experience intense dissatisfaction and consider making a career change.

Career changing, in fact, is becoming more popular with all job searchers, especially those aged 30 to 60 undergoing volatile job changes. According to the Bureau of Labor Statistics, the average worker will change careers two to three times throughout his or her career.

But whether you hate your job and contemplate a career change or are looking for your first serious job and don't have a clue about which career path to take, it all spells career crisis. The process of self-discovery and information gathering is pretty much the same.

Should I Do It Myself or Seek Professional Help?

Two methods exist for finding a career you love: the old-fashioned school of soul searching, self-discovery, and experimentation or the new path of obtaining professional help and career counseling.

Which is better? I'll cop out and take the "Fifth." It depends on you. Personally, I'm more inclined to try the go-it-alone path first.

CAUTIONARY NOTE: Be prepared to blunder, stumble, and test some paths that may lead nowhere. Not everyone is willing to do that. It's no crime if you're not willing to try it. For whatever reason, many job seekers can't spare a millisecond of time. If you don't have the time to look deep inside yourself for answers, it's no crime to turn to a qualified career counselor. More on that later. First, let's try doing it ourselves with some painless exercises that could open exciting career doors. For most people, all it takes to find career passion is time, insight, and a sense of adventure.

Who Am I and What Can I Do? Eight Fun Exercises to Help You Find a Job You Love

Exercise 1: Write Job Summaries

Depending on how many jobs you've had throughout your career, try to summarize the highlights of each one. Don't panic. This isn't half as difficult as it sounds. To make the process easier, use a current résumé as a guide so you can see the progression of events in black-and-white before you. I urge you, however, to go beyond your résumé (a concept which I'm going to debunk later on with great relish). If you've been working for more than 10 years, chances are every job you've held is not included on your résumé. Naturally, you've left out many of the insignificant positions so you don't confuse employers or become labeled as a "job hopper."

This logic made sense when you wrote your résumé, but for your job summaries, *including all* your jobs (or just those that you can recall accurately) is important. Before you throw your hands in the air in frustration, this is not a book-length exercise. You should, however, highlight those events that stick out in your mind. That will give you a broad panorama from which to choose.

How much space should you allow for each job? As much as necessary. An insignificant summer job in which you earned money to help pay for your college education is barely worth including. A short entry may look like this: "Arctic Snowsuit Factory—for 3 months I loaded crates of snowsuits, filling orders for the upcoming fall season. The job was hard and boring. Horrendous experience. I did it to earn enough to cover my tuition for the next college semester." Nothing more needs to be said. Factory work is not your calling; move on.

As with your résumé, use a chronological listing in recounting each job history. Start from the moment you graduated high school or college and work forward. When discussing each job, include what you liked, disliked, and learned, and your accomplishments. For instance:

> *1975–1978. Ding-a-Ling Widgets, Ltd.*—One of the pioneer widget companies to produce widgets on a national scale. Learned a great deal about the intricate design components and the handcrafted elements of each widget. The best part of the job was I worked with two of the finest widget designers in the world. Working with them closely on a daily basis was the highlight of my 3-year stay with the company.

For a small company, it was awfully bureaucratic. I found it hard to develop my own ideas. Management was virtually inaccessible. Worse yet, it was more apt to consider the ideas and designs of senior engineers over mine, which often were equally good and sometimes a lot better. As a result, I threw in the towel, giving up on what I felt were great ideas because I didn't feel like grappling with the red tape.

The problem was the company wasn't aggressive enough. Instead of trying to be one step ahead of the times, it barely kept pace. Despite these shortcomings, I learned a great deal about the widget industry and became a first-rate designer. I learned to think for myself and most important to fight for an idea in which I believe. In the long run, if you won't stand up for your ideas, no one else will.

Now do you get the idea?

After you've finished writing each job summary, capsulize your results using the following headings (short-term, summer, part-time, or interim jobs need not be included):

1. I liked the job because...
2. I disliked the job because...
3. I learned...
4. My accomplishments were...
5. Skills acquired included...

In the above summary, your headings might look like this:

1. I liked the job because it gave me a global picture of how the widget industry worked and insights into how widgets are designed.
2. I disliked the job because I wasn't allowed to express my creativity. I found it difficult to play the bureaucratic game.
3. I learned how large corporations function and how widgets are designed, manufactured, and mass-produced.

4. My accomplishments were surviving in a high-powered company and contributing my talents to streamline the widget's design.
5. Polished skills I already had; I acquired no new skills.

Exercise 2: Rewrite the Past

For the next two exercises we're going to harness our imaginations and have some fun in the bargain. Here's your opportunity to go back in time and erase what you disliked and highlight what you loved.

Instead of going back to every job you had, you're going to throw all your jobs into a big pot and simmer away the fat, leaving only the experiences you want to highlight. Then you'll rewrite them the way you would have liked to experience them. Don't rack your brain trying to recall every incident. Instead, use your job summaries as a guide or departure point to rewrite experiences to your liking.

If a number of jobs were less than memorable and you wish you'd never held them in the first place, little or nothing needs to be said. For instance, if you want to let off steam, an entry like the following might make you feel better:

> If I had it to do all again, I never would have taken the job at Diddle-Do Machine Guns, Inc. I wasted an entire year of my life. Management amounted to a bunch of spoiled high-grade morons who didn't know whether they were coming or going. Most of the workers were gutless yes-men who'd do anything to hold on to their jobs.

After an entry like that, there's nothing left to say. Maybe you took the job because you needed money to get yourself out of debt or because nothing else was in the offing. Needless to say, your job summary and capsulization made it more than clear that you had a negative, unproductive experience. Take the hint and move on to the next situation. By process of elimination, you're learning about yourself.

If the imaginary person who worked for Ding-a-Ling Widgets were to rewrite his or her 3-year stay, it might look something like this:

> *1975–1978. Ding-a-Ling Widgets, Ltd.*—My experience at Ding-a-Ling turned out to be a major starting point for my career. Since the company recognized my talents, I got my first real break. It was an honor to work with two of the best widget designers worldwide. They took me under their wings, encouraged me, and taught me. It wasn't long before I, too, became a prominent force in my company. Once they recognized my design capabilities, I was given free rein. Unlike in other companies, I had no trouble getting to senior managers and convincing them my ideas were marketable. It was a great feeling not having to contend with miles of red tape and to be appreciated for my abilities.

By rewriting the above exercise, this imaginary worker got a chance to correct deficits on prior jobs and identify the stumbling blocks that inhibited his or her creativity. By doing this simple cathartic exercise, you have the opportunity to see the difference between what you actually did and what you would have liked to have done. It points to what you want in the future.

That wasn't so bad, was it? Are repressed thoughts, feelings, and ideas beginning to bubble to the surface? I bet they are. Let's go on.

Exercise 3: Create a Fantasy Job

Along the lines of the above exercise, we're going to create the job of jobs, the one we think about in secret moments, possibly just before we doze off to sleep.

Exercise 2 set the tone; now we're going to depart from reality and tap into our fantasy lives. Once the task is completed, we'll take a look at our fantasy jobs and see how far they depart from reality.

Again, don't feel you have to fill a certain amount of space. It doesn't matter whether it takes a paragraph or a page or two to describe your fantasy job in detail.

Let's look at two examples. The first is the fantasy of a cosmetics salesperson working for a large Detroit department store.

> The fantasy job is one where I could come and go as I pleased. I'd be president of a large company employing hundreds of people. I'd be in command and everyone would answer to me. I'd have final say concerning everything that went on within my company. My annual salary would be more than $200,000 and I'd have a limousine and company car at my disposal at all times. The best part is I wouldn't have to watch every penny and budget everything I earn, as I do know. As head of my own company, I could buy anything I want without batting an eyelash. The job would also give me unlimited mobility. I'd go everywhere—the Caribbean in the winter, Paris in the spring, you name it.

Quite a fantasy, isn't it? Do you wish you had a job like the above? Let's go on, do one more, and then compare the two fantasies. The next is from a computer salesperson in Oregon.

> My fantasy job is having my own automotive repair shop specializing in expensive foreign cars. Ever since I was a teenager, I've been an avid car nut. From high school on, I've always tinkered with cars. In fact, when I was 26, I practically built my own sports car from parts I found in junkyards. It was a labor of love. Once you get involved in expensive sports cars, you're hooked forever. I've spent years studying the technology and the workmanship that goes into Ferraris, Porsches, Jaguars, and the like, and I find it a nonstop learning experience. You never get tired of working on these incredible machines. Beyond that, the idea of running my own business and not having to answer to anyone is an exhilarating thought. I'd love to find a way to pull it off because I know I can make a go of it.

Now let's compare the two fantasies. Which one has a greater chance of actually being realized? If you said number 2, you get the prize.

Let's take a quick detour and explain about fantasies. Fantasizing is normal. Better yet, it's a lot of fun. You can fantasize about anything you like. If you commit a crime, you risk paying a fine or going to jail. If you are late for work 2 weeks straight or don't show up for a month, I guarantee you'll be fired. But fantasize about committing the perfect crime or telling off your boss and coming and going as you like and nothing will happen. That's the nice part about fantasies. You can hitch a ride in a spacecraft and circle the universe for an hour or two, find a million dollars on a street corner, or be president of the United States. The enjoyable part is living and experiencing it vicariously; the bad part is it's only a fantasy, never to see the light of day.

Now, back to the two fantasies cited above. They clearly demonstrate two distinct types of fantasies: the unrealistic and realistic variety. The first one is inaccessible, the second is realizable.

Go back and read them both again. The woman who wrote the first fantasy was far removed from her dream. Although it's certainly not impossible for a cosmetics salesperson to become the president of a company, what's missing in this description are the facts. The descriptions are vague and aimless. Throughout the fantasy paragraph, the salesperson never once mentions the type of company or plans to run it. The fantasy spotlights a big salary, perks, and the fun and power of jetting around the globe in overwhelming luxury. The fantasy is about the money, not the work.

Can this person connect the fantasy to real life in order to isolate particles of truth, seeds for further development? Unfortunately, no.

But the computer salesperson's fantasy falls into the realistic category. By connecting the fantasy to real life, the person would see that it's no surprise that his fascination with mechanical devices had branched out in new directions, such as expensive sports cars. With this background and inclinations, wanting to own an automotive repair shop catering to expensive sports cars is not beyond reach. If the person didn't know anything about sports cars, it would be a different matter. But having grown up around cars, with grease permanently embedded underneath his fingernails, he is voicing a fantasy that has some validity. Not to say that it would be easy. Having the mechanical aptitude is only a first step. Many problems would have to be overcome, such as learning how to start and run a business, not to mention having the temperament and attitude of an entrepreneur.

The telling question is: Could it be done under the right circumstances and conditions? Absolutely!

This brings us to your fantasies. Now that you know the difference between a realistic and unrealistic fantasy, where does yours fall? If your fantasy is unrealistic, what could be done to bring it into a realistic realm? If it's finding an attaché case filled with a million dollars behind a tree in a remote wooded area, the fantasy should be abandoned.

A career change, while it might require difficult maneuvers, has to be realistic and attainable. Whether you're 100 percent sure about the change or only vaguely certain, great value can result from connecting your personal experiences and present career with the proposed change. Most career changers who have thoroughly worked out the details of the change, or have at least realized that the change is attainable, harbor fantasies grounded in personal experience. The computer salesperson, for instance, can actually change careers if he is able to acquire the skills necessary to pull it off.

One final question you must ask yourself: If your fantasy contains seeds of truth, what skills must be acquired to actually realize that change?

If the computer salesperson were to answer this question, the response would be: knowledge of financing, retailing, organizational skills for running a business, and interpersonal skills for dealing with colleagues and staff.

Take a breather. The next exercise requires no heavy thinking or writing. All you need is a newspaper and a pencil.

Exercise 4: Cull the Classifieds

Get a hold of the employment section of your daily newspaper and make a list of the all the jobs that appeal to you and that you might consider doing, whether you are qualified or not. Better than the weekday paper is the Sunday employment section, which is the fattest of the week. You'll be surprised at how much fun this is.

Incredibly enough, most job searchers seldom thumb through the entire employment section. Usually, they hurriedly fumble to the job categories they think they're qualified for and ignore the rest. But when you go through the entire section, you'll discover other jobs of interest. Who's to say you may not have some or all of the qualifications required?

An example that comes to mind is a mechanical engineer who decided to abandon engineering and become a full-time writer. He hoped to eventually earn his living as a fiction writer, but until he was established, he could keep body and soul together through technical writing. With his background he had the credentials. Initially, he searched for technical writing jobs under the "Writing" category and was surprised to find not many listed. What he failed to consider was that they might have been listed under other headings. When he scoured the paper from beginning to end, he found a plethora of technical writing jobs under the "Engineering," "Technical," "Editorial," and "Computer" headings. He learned a valuable lesson: Use ingenuity and common sense when searching for something. Seek and you shall find.

Surprisingly, this exercise takes longer than expected. You'll start out thinking that you'll jump through the employment section in a matter of minutes; but once you begin, you'll find yourself pondering over jobs. "That looks kind of interesting!" "I never considered doing that, but I know I can." "I have many of the qualifications they're looking for." You may discover some strange job titles which appeal to you and for which you're qualified. Approach this task with an open mind and let your list run as long as you like. At the very end, you may have 10, 20, or possibly 30 different jobs that turn you on.

General List of Interesting Jobs

1.
2.

3.
4.
5.
6.
7.
8.
9.
10.

The next task involves doing some selective weeding to create two new lists: one that contains jobs in which you're very interested and another made up of jobs in which you're only casually interested.

Jobs of High Interest Value	*Jobs of Moderate Interest Value*
1.	1.
2.	2.
3.	3.
4.	4.
5.	5.
6.	6.
7.	7.
8.	8.
9.	9.
10.	10.

The list is getting smaller, isn't it? But I bet it's still too long. You say you have 25 jobs on your list? Far too many. A still more challenging task is creating two more lists: jobs that can be done with little or no retraining and others that require intensive retraining.

Jobs Requiring Little to No Retraining

1.
2.
3.
4.

5.
6.
7.
8.
9.
10.

Jobs Requiring Intensive Retraining

1.
2.
3.
4.
5.
6.
7.
8.
9.
10.

Now you're getting a clearer picture of where you stand. To be absolutely accurate, go back to the two lists you just put together and add the following headings under each list: "Skills You Possess" and "Skills You Need."

Skills You Possess	*Skills You Need*
1.	1.
2.	2.
3.	3.
4.	4.
5.	5.
6.	6.

The picture is getting even sharper, isn't it? Suddenly, you feel much better. Naturally, there will be an awful lot of things you're not equipped to do, but there will also be a lot of things you can do with either little or intensive training. In other words, new options are popping up all over the place.

Now, let's put our thinking caps back on and do another creative exercise.

Exercise 5: Uncover the Fusion Factor

You're thinking, "What the heck does this mean? This guy has gone off the deep end. How does he think up these terms?" Relax, it's not half as complicated as you think.

Too many of us meander through life, seldom thinking about what motivates us, why we do things and why we like certain things and detest others. It is interesting to note that just as themes run through novels, poems, and essays, they also run through our lives. This is where the "fusion factor" enters the picture. Simply put, it's the consistent stream or binding factor (or factors) running through our lives. We may not be aware of it, but we're fairly logical creatures. Even though we've done many different things, worked for many employers, attended several schools, and met many people, consistent themes run through our lives and they'll continue to do so until the day we die. While our lives change daily, there is an element of consistency we can count on. If we peer into the future and try to imagine what we'll be doing 20 years from now, certain elements of our personality and psychological makeup will remain the same. This is the fusion factor, those elements that fuse our lives and maintain a sense of constancy within all of us.

The more you think about the fusion factor, the faster you'll see the connection to your career change. Even though you're preparing to break new ground and tread on new career terrain, some elements will never change and will carry with you from one career to another, no matter how radical your career change.

To isolate the fusion factor, carve your life into three distinct parts: early years, education/training years, and future perception. Get a pencil and paper and do the following short exercise. For each of these life parts, free-associate, quickly jotting down the first thing that comes to mind. Speed is of the essence when free-associating. It's those first thoughts that open locked doors to your subconscious. They reveal desires, thoughts, emotions, and feelings. Be honest. Even if it makes no sense at all, jot it down. It can be anything from past or present memories (pleasant or unpleasant) to noteworthy events, highlights, victories, losses, and fantasies. Let your mind wander into the atmosphere and land wherever it cares to. You have free rein.

When I asked a 45-year-old accountant to do this exercise, the first things he jotted down under the "early years" heading were lawns, mountains, outside, green, and air. When he got to the second part (education/training years), he listed routines, conformity, discipline, rules, structure, confinement, duty, and responsibility. And for the third item, future perception, he listed security, routines, boredom, sameness, and confinement.

Does that not tell us something about this person's feelings about life and work? It doesn't tell us about his hidden skills, but it tells us things no less valuable.

Within each part of his life, a pervasive theme emerges, revealing unmet needs and disillusionment, all pointing to an overwhelming desire to change his situation. What exactly does this accountant want? You don't have to be a psychoanalyst to know that he has a compelling need to add something to his life, something he enjoyed in his childhood. When he freely associated about the early years, he listed nature terms, all of which spell freedom and openness. But for the remaining two parts, he withdrew, as if he'd walked into a dark monastery and closed the door on the world. Instead of the feeling of openness that was present during his childhood, there is a claustrophobic feeling about his life, a turning off or turning inward, closing part of himself, thus limiting the sense of enjoyment that he should be deriving from life and work.

Put it all together and we have a clear fusion factor for this accountant. It is a compelling need to break out and express himself openly and be uninhibited. The fusing element of his life is a rigidity that has acted like a vise, not allowing him to experience life fully.

Do the constant references to the outside and the use of words like *green, air,* and *mountains* mean that he should give up accounting and become a forester, hunter/trapper, or farmer? Not necessarily. What it points to is a need to find something that gives him a feeling of freedom, not necessarily working outdoors.

In uncovering this man's fusion factor, we find that the theme running through his life is a weighty sadness and a need to give himself something he hasn't experienced since he was a child. However, like so many of us, he ambled through life, barely making thought-out decisions that would have a positive effect on his life. Whether he chose accountancy or was nudged into it by a well-meaning parent or close relative is irrelevant. The point is he chose it because he felt it would make him happy and give him what he needed. He chose security, a key to a successful life in which he could have the things he thought were important. But did he ever sit down and say to himself, "What is it I really want to do with my life? What will make me happy?" Most probably, no. If he had asked himself these questions, the next logical step would be translating and applying his answers to the real world. In sum, once he finds what excites him, the next logical step is finding a vocation that will give it to him.

Asking yourself the above questions seems only logical, right? But how many of us are logical? We often let other motives (the pressing need for a well-paying job to cover our bills and support a family, pressure from family, the compulsion to find so-called respectable, prestigious work) guide us to the careers we ultimately pick.

Remember what I said earlier. It's a whole new job market out there. For our fathers and grandfathers, a job was a survival maneuver. Even if they didn't like the work, they accepted it and did the best they could.

Even though our career plights are better today, it doesn't take a decade of psychoanalysis to know that our expectations about life and work are not very different from those of our ancestors. Even though the world spins frantically on its axis with technology creating new career options, many of us do things from a conservative and close-minded perspective.

Exercise 6: Examine What Turns You on About Life

You can take the easy way out on this one and simply compile a list. But if I were you, I'd try the essay. Since no one else is going to read it, a literary effort is not needed. The process of writing down your thoughts in a coherent fashion can trigger great ideas and rev up your creative wheels in the process.

A few hints before beginning. Think total. In other words, don't limit yourself to things that excite you about the work you do or would like to do. Focus on life in general. It's not just Monday through Friday you're going to be writing about, but Saturday and Sunday as well.

Along with work-related passions, discuss your part-time job, interests, or hobbies.

One approach is to start with something general—you'll automatically gravitate toward the more specific. Another possibility is to consider a hobby or part-time passion and see where it takes you. A former corporate executive who opened up a small country furniture refinishing business wrote this:

> Ever since I was a kid, I enjoyed working with my hands. It gave me no end of pleasure taking a piece of wood and whittling it into shape. As a teenager, I started doing simple carpentry around the house and I even earned money doing it part-time. But it never occurred to me that I could actually earn a living with my hands. So I pursued a business and within a relatively short period of time became very successful, going through a number of jobs until I became a senior executive of a national food-distributing company. But while I was carving a career for myself, I spent all my spare time working with furniture—stripping, rebuilding, and refinishing it. When it became the only thing that turned me on and there was really nothing else I wanted to do, I figured it was time to make the move and open my own refinishing shop.

It's not half as bad as it sounds. Once you get going, thoughts will automatically roll from your head on to the paper. After all, what's so difficult about discussing something close to your heart, the thing (or things) that excite you?

Once you've finished, create another column and list the skills or interests, or both, highlighted in your essay.

In the above example, the corporate executive turned furniture refinisher concentrated on his skills as follows:

Skills Isolated

1. Ability to work with hands in building and refinishing furniture
2. Ability to conceptualize and visualize a project from start to finish

Interests Isolated

1. Enjoy studying and collecting books and magazines on traditional furniture-refinishing techniques

Here is an example of a person who was able to turn his skills into a career.

However, while you may be passionate about interests and hobbies, it may not always be so easy to translate them into careers.

If your essay revolved around your passionate interest in books and how easily you can while away entire days reading, it doesn't mean you'll be happy as a librarian. Your temperament and personality may not be suited to the work. Or if you're an avid hunter, ask yourself if it is possible to become a professional hunter. It's not that you couldn't become a professional hunter by moving to Africa, the Canadian wilds, or a similar faraway place, but that the odds are against such a switch. Not because work is so difficult to find (which it is) and the lifestyle is so precarious (which it is), but more practically, because you don't have the temperament for the change. It's one thing to go out and hunt deer, pheasant, and wild ducks with your cronies on weekends; it's another thing to become a professional hunter and go trekking to the far corners of the earth in search of game. The first is only a sport; the second requires a radical lifestyle change.

Think clearly and pragmatically about your interests in terms of careers. An avid stamp collector (philatelist) may derive intense pleasure, tucked away in a den for a weekend, researching and studying stamps, but he or she might go crazy doing it full-time. That goes for countless other hobbies and interests.

Summing up, we all have interests and hobbies occupying our spare time. To place them within the context of our lives, we must see them for what they are. Ask yourself why you enjoy these activities and what it is that gives you pleasure. Is it intellectual challenge, physical exercise, excitement, or simply a change of pace? The answer will show you whether your interest or hobby stands a chance of occupying a more prominent place in your life. If it does become more than a weekend pursuit—if you find yourself immersed in it at odd hours (early in the morning or late in the evening) and your thoughts are consumed by it throughout the day—your interest should be seriously investigated.

When a hobby or interest becomes the focal point of your life, it's time to do something about it and seriously investigate the possibility of changing careers.

Exercise 7: Write Your Obituary

After getting this far, you must be convinced I have now gone off the deep end. I bet I can read your mind. "This guy is absolutely nuts. How can I write my obituary if I'm still alive and not even halfway through my life?"

These good questions point to the very reason for doing it. The fact that you are alive gives this exercise meaning. Having applied yourself in a number of other exercises, you now have a pretty good understanding of your past and present. But what about the future? You've rewritten your past as you would have liked to have lived it; now it's time to think about what lies ahead. Hurl yourself into the future, fantasize about your death, and imagine reading your obituary as you would like it to read, having accomplished everything you wanted to during your life. The exercise doesn't seem so silly now, does it? You can then translate this into the mainstream of your life.

Yes, it's a grim topic. Yet all of us, at some point, think about death. We ponder about friends and loved ones dying and we even fantasize about our own death. You've probably thought about how you would like to die, maybe even when and where. Not pleasant thoughts, but they're real nevertheless and shouldn't be discounted. By the same token, you've fantasized about accomplishing certain things before you die. Now it's time to unearth those thoughts and look at them in the light of day.

What are you going to say? Which traits, characteristics, and accomplishments do you want people to remember? When your time comes, for what would you like to be admired?

Give your obituary a lot of thought before writing it. Give it a slipshod treatment and you're only cheating yourself. If you delve into it, a brighter picture emerges, a three-dimensional vision in which past, present, and future meld into a meaningful whole. Suddenly you realize all the things you haven't done and want to accomplish. You're aware of your mortality; you realize that you have just so much time left. Sounds morbid, but again, these are realistic, mature thoughts.

A medical technician seriously thinking about going back to school to become a physician said he experienced an overwhelming feeling of excitement when he completed his obituary.

"It sounded like a morbid idea before I started it," he said, "but once I began to take it seriously, it wasn't long before I really got into it. I found that I was thinking about translating my fantasies into reality. Unanswered questions occurred to me like 'Why couldn't I do that?' Maybe it would take 4 or 5 years to make the switch, but it could be done, since I have the appropriate background and foundation."

When he completed the obituary, he wrote what hopefully will be an accurate description of the last leg of his life. Afterward, he reported feeling energized and raring to go. The feeling was, "What am I waiting for? I must begin immediately."

Writing your obituary is a personal exercise, so don't feel you have to show it to anyone. Many people I've spoken to didn't care to share their thoughts about the future. A few said it might be a jinx to realize their goals. The idea is to learn and benefit from the exercise: If you accomplish that, it is worth the effort.

Exercise 8: Create a Fallback Position

Start thinking about a fallback position for yourself, just in case everything doesn't work out as planned. What happens if your plans go awry and circumstances beyond your control prevent you from achieving your career switch? You've learned new things about yourself, gotten in touch with new vocational/professional skills, and isolated a battery of marketable, transferable skills. Now is the time to arm yourself with a strong fallback position, and if you want to be doubly secure, why not choose two or three related fields? The more thought you give to contingency plans, the greater your chances of never having to abandon your career change and return to a job you hate.

Finding Professional Help

All isn't lost if you were dissatisfied with the above results. If none of the previous exercises proved insightful and you're still confused about which career path to take, find a trained professional who can guide you to a rewarding career.

Consider these valuable pointers for finding the most qualified counselor

1. *Acquaint yourself with the terminology.* Check your local paper and you'll see ads for a variety of career services. The people who run them call themselves by such names as career counselors, career managers, career management consultants, career guidance professionals, career guidance executives, retirement advisers, recruitment consultants, executive search professionals, and professional career consultants. Similarly, outplacement centers provide "termination assistance" for people who have been fired from supervisory, middle-management, and upper-management

positions. Outplacement centers are hired on a contract basis by companies to provide a battery of services to help terminated workers find new jobs. Understandably, companies feel it's poor public relations to coldly dismiss employees without letting them down gently and helping them find new positions. If it's a reputable, well-established outplacement organization, the services provided are sophisticated and expensive. The center tests, evaluates, and interviews the terminated worker to find the right situation. After a battery of test results is analyzed, a career change may be indicated. The outplacement firm helps the client execute the change. The best part is that the in-transition worker pays nothing for the service.

The majority of us, however, require professional career assistance and, predictably, have to foot the bill. So use discretion. Don't put too much stock in high-falutin' titles, because that's all they are.

2. *Be wary of newspaper ads for career counselors.* Want ads can be the least effective method of finding a competent professional. You don't find attorneys or doctors by scouring the Yellow Pages or the classified section of your newspaper. Beware of enticing come-on phrases such as "access to the hidden job market," "our sophisticated database has all the jobs you've dreamed of," "our contacts can open doors you can't open yourself," and "change your life." A reputable career counselor doesn't have to resort to gimmick advertising.
3. *Make a list of 5 to 10 career professionals who might be able to help you.* Plan on visiting at least three firms, better yet five, so you have a basis for comparison. Instead of randomly stopping in to see each one, call to find out something about their services. Ask general questions about their services and whether they provide a free consultation. If they charge for a consultation or are overly insistent upon meeting you before volunteering any information over the phone, thank them for their time and cross them off your list. They're not for you. Career counselors should be more than happy to provide as much information as they can over

the phone. The majority of reputable career counselors will give you a free consultation lasting anywhere from 15 to 30 minutes.

4. *What do they charge?* It's impossible to present a realistic range of prices. Fees can range from a very modest $50 an hour up into the thousands for a complete program. Don't equate a high charge with quality. You can pay over $3000 for a comprehensive workshop with individual coaching that can last 2 months and have your life rejuvenated in the process. Or you can be in the same place you started, only $3000 poorer. Contingent upon your budget, the question is: What exactly do you get for your money? If the career expert can't provide a number of intelligent answers, you know what you have to do.

   Heed this advice from business magazine *Fast Company:* "Never do business with a career counselor who expects big up-front fees. Any respectable counselor is prepared to charge on an hourly basis. No respectable counselor demands long-term contracts or guaranteed payments. You can get serious career advice from a highly regarded expert for a total investment of $450 to $750."

5. *Beware of guarantees.* As much as you'd love a big brother or sister relationship, think clearly. If the counselor makes exaggerated guarantees, promising you a better job, new outlook, lifestyle, and the like, be wary. Think about it for a couple of seconds. Not knowing you—your capabilities, outlook, goals, and marketability—how can he or she possibly guarantee anything?

   According to the late John Crystal, coauthor of *Where Do I Go from Here with My Life?*, the real problem is not so much helping someone find another job, which so many counseling firms try to do, as helping someone discover who he or she is in order to make intelligent career decisions. Once people discover who they are, they can begin to realize their potential.

6. *Is the program compatible?* Once you are face-to-face with the career counselor, ask him or her to spell out exactly what the program is all about to ascertain if it meets your needs. Take notes so you can ponder the information at your leisure. Find out about

the firm's background and ask yourself questions: "Can this person actually help me? Does the program make sense or am I being conned with flowery hype?"

7. *Beware of high-pressure tactics.* If the person tries to rush you, acts evasive, and is intent on having you sign on the dotted line before leaving, grab your attaché case and head out the door. Many less-than-reputable career counselors are expert at creating a sense of urgency, subtly intimidating you into signing up for their crash course "which will put you back to work within 3 weeks."

   Beware of such unsavory tactics. Picking the right career counselor is as important as picking the right shrink. Both of these professionals play a major part in your life. A bad decision can delay, hinder, or confuse you, not to mention put a severe dent in your pocketbook.
8. *Go with your instincts.* Keep your radar on at all times. Aside from critically watching and listening, pay attention to your other senses as well—the senses that can't be easily defined, yet warn of pending danger or compromising situations. In other words, pay attention to the vibrations generated by the place. What do they tell you about the people and place? What is the atmosphere like? If you're going to pay for the services of a career counselor, you should feel positive vibrations as soon as you walk in the door.
9. *Don't make a hasty decision.* Once you've visited a number of career counselors, spend a couple of days thinking about which one you'd like to work with. Replay each interview, considering what each counselor said and weighing one against the other, and you'll have the ammunition to make a sound decision—one that is right for you.

Let's move on down that lonesome career highway and find out who can be trusted.

CHAPTER 6

TRUST NO ONE: PARANOIA IS HEALTHY

RULE 6 Take control of your own life. Don't let anyone do it for you.

Jerry Rubin, the outspoken student rebel of the 1960s, said, "Trust no one over 30."

That was a hostile remark. But back in that turbulent decade, it made sense. Yes, it was a rash and irresponsible statement, yet it captured the energy of the moment. Rubin's real message was: "Question everything, stand up and fight for what you believe in, and rely on your own intuition."

Rubin was telling young people not to sell out and buy in to a complacent social and corporate culture hell-bent on maintaining the status quo.

If you're wondering why I went off on this nostalgic trip back to the 1960s, it's because I want you to adopt a similar attitude. I'm taking paranoia to its outer limits. It's not to make you overly suspicious so you're constantly looking over your shoulder. Paranoia keeps you in shape, tense, suspicious, questioning, and ready for the unexpected.

Don't get me wrong. I'm simply conveying an attitude that screams, "Take control of your own life. Don't let anyone do it for you." Pick the cliché that hits the bull's-eye: Chart your own course, run your own race, and don't let anyone carry the ball for you. In short, do it yourself. Take responsibility for your own life and career. If you screw up, it's no one's fault but your own. That's the cleanest and sharpest code of living. It's also the simplest.

Combine healthy paranoia with the jungle tactics mentioned earlier and you'll become an unstoppable machine, efficiently spiraling toward your target—a great job—at warp speed.

Trust Your Instincts

Once you're suspicious, distrusting, and questioning, you won't accept everything dished out to you. And you won't become apathetic, indifferent, or lazy. That's the trap our ancestors' generations fell into. Complacency is the enemy because it stops you dead in your tracks. The folks who get jobs quickly trust their instincts. I urge you to do the same. Start by taking nothing at face value.

Cynics, skeptics, and questioners cross the finish line first. Remember what I said in the introduction. Everything is different. The prototypical American corporation of the 1940s and 1950s has been replaced by slimmer, faster, chameleonlike organizations that can stop, start, turn, and swerve on a dime. Speed is of the essence and loyalty is dead.

REMEMBER: An employer owes you nothing but a fair shake, which translates to decent pay and benefits. If you're lucky, the company will recognize your talents and reward you appropriately. Don't expect security or a future. The most you can hope for is short-term security. Anything else is a gift.

Employers want people who can stand on their own two feet and think for themselves. Sing the party line and you are useless.

Beware of the Three Biggest Employer Lies

Think about making a speedy exit as soon as an employer says:

1. You've got a future with us.
2. We're all one big happy family.
3. We take good care of our people.

The employer is lying to you. And it may not be intentional either. Many brainwashed bureaucrats who've been in one place for a long time actually believe it. But most spout these three lies because they know job searchers love hearing them. It makes job seekers feel secure, like they found the perfect home. This is it, a place to hang out for the next 30 years.

Forget the effect these hollow lines have on you. Ask yourself if there is any truth to them. Better yet, ask yourself how on earth they could possibly be true. Welcome to the 1990s, when a healthy degree of paranoia is the best life preserver you can find.

Success hinges on your ability to take control of your life and pilot your own ship. As soon as you do so, you're in the driver's seat and in control of your own destiny. Fate and luck play a part in everyone's future, but 90 percent of what we achieve in life hinges on ourselves and what we put into this crazy game called life.

Let's get our act in tow by creating a job-hunting machine.

CHAPTER 7

WHO ARE YOU CALLING DISORGANIZED?

RULE 7 Fine-tune your job-hunting machine.

Management gurus make a big deal over the importance of being organized. They make you think everyone is born with an organization gene.

Wrong! The truth is most people are disorganized. That includes myself. Feel better? It doesn't take much effort to be disorganized either. All you have to do is follow your instincts.

Beware of Morning Talk Shows and Afternoon Soap Operas

One of the biggest obstacles job hunters face is working out of their home. It would be ideal to run your job search out of an office. Unfortunately, that's a luxury most of us can't afford. Like it or not, we're forced to work from our home and deal with the traps and addictions tempting us to goof off.

The archenemy of consistent job hunting is *comfort.* My downfall was television. As soon as I woke up, I snapped on the boob tube and then struggled to turn it off again. I'd start by flipping on the *Today Show* to find out what the weather was like and then I'd get involved in all their stories. Suddenly, I was entranced by some guy who spent 85 years in the Himalayas searching for the meaning of life, followed by a 2-minute spot about fast-food being good for you. What a relief knowing I could power up for a heavy afternoon of job hunting with a Whopper, fries, and a shake.

You get the idea. It's easy to get hooked on morning shows. Like most veteran TV addicts, as soon as a commercial comes on, I mindlessly begin channel surfing. And if you've got cable, providing 40 or more channels from which to choose, it's hard to tear yourself away. Before I realized, it was 10 a.m., 2 hours into the precious morning, and I was riveted to a documentary about little-known Caribbean islands fast becoming the new vacation spot. "Why that's perfect," I said to myself. "When I get a job, that's where I am going to take my next vacation." Naturally, I failed to tell myself that if I never get out of the house and start job hunting, that will never happen.

If you don't apply the brakes, it will be 2:30 p.m. and you'll still be propped in front of the tube, rumpled, in your pajamas, clutching the remote control with a can of beer and a jumbo bag of potato chips at your side.

The next biggest problem is the refrigerator, that towering box holding a cornucopia of delectables. When you're home, you don't have to call the deli around the corner to send up a BLT, coffee, and a piece of chocolate cake. You just amble into the kitchen and your favorite high-calorie munchies are neatly arranged in one place. And don't forget about the microwave oven, every lazy person's downfall. In less than 5 minutes, the neat machine can turn out a sumptuous feast.

Those are just two of the perils of being home. Beware of other traps, too, such as sleeping too late and getting hooked on goof-off projects that have nothing to do with job hunting, like painting the house, fixing the shed, and cleaning out the attic.

Now for the heavy Freudian interpretation. We kill time to avoid job hunting, a labor-intensive task triggering anxiety. Brilliant, right? It can be likened to being in school and creating endless stall tactics to avoid writing a term paper.

Sound familiar? If you've been out of work a long time, I bet I have struck a familiar chord.

Get Tough on Yourself
Job Hunting Is a Full-Time Job

Don't beat yourself up because you've gone to creative ends to avoid job hunting. It's normal. Maybe no one told you that job hunting requires real work: It's not just mail out résumés, make a few calls, and wait for the phone to ring. It takes a concentrated effort, strategy, and lots of pavement pounding. Welcome to job hunting in the 1990s. Regardless of what your cronies told you, most job hunters give lip service to the job-hunting process and barely commit themselves to the task.

I guarantee you'll feel a lot better once you get your act together. You won't even miss the tube.

The solution is *discipline*—the first step toward organizing your job-hunting routines. Start by applying the brakes on all those nasty addictions stalling the job-hunting process.

Ask yourself an obvious question: If you had to report to a job, could you goof off? *Solution:* Think of job hunting as a full-time job. That means being ready to go to work no later than 8 a.m. every morning, 5 days a week. It means no TV or obsessive snacking.

Once your job-hunting act is off the ground, you'll be pleasantly surprised to discover you're getting up early—charged, motivated, and raring to go. That's a hell of a good feeling.

First order of business: Set up a place to work. Call it your command center. This is your private area where you'll strategize your hunt and store all your tools. Consider these tips

1. *Avoid makeshift offices.* You're asking for trouble if you try to run your job search out of an attaché case. Within 2 weeks you'll be drowning in paper and pulling out your hair. The upshot will be crippling disorganization, which leads to missed opportunities.

2. *Create a permanent space.* I'm not talking about renting a spacious carpeted office complete with a sprawling mahogany desk, computer, fax, multiple phone lines, copier, and secretary with an IQ of 190. That's a fantasy. Most of us will have to content ourselves with something less grand. The truth is you don't need a high-tech office. A partitioned corner of a living room, attic, or basement will do just fine. All that counts is that it's quiet and can be permanent for the duration of your job search.

   Once you have a place to work, consider buying these essential tools:

   - *Answering machine.* Don't attempt to carry on without one. It's as important as your wallet, pocketbook, or keys. Can you risk missing a call from a potential employer about a hot job lead? Answering machines are cheap. You don't need a top-of-the-line model replete with attached phone fax or printer. You can pick up last year's model for $50 or less in a discount office supply store. Whichever unit you buy, make sure it has a remote call-in feature so you can check your messages from the field.
   - *Organizer.* Praise the genius who invented the portable day organizer. Efficient job hunters wouldn't go anywhere without their portable organizers containing calendar, planning diary, and notepad. The nifty, inexpensive gadget organizes your life.
   - *Bulletin board.* If you are the messy room type and were the kind of kid who wouldn't clean up his room even if he faced a firing squad, I urge you to spring for a bulletin board. The bigger the better. Its purpose is to tack up critical appointments, reminders, messages, affirmations—whatever—in front of your nose. Important reminders can get buried on a desk, but you can't miss them if they're staring you in the face. My rule of thumb is the bigger I print the reminder, the more important the message. When you're preparing for a big appointment, it's easy to forget something critical, such as a letter of recommendation, a project, proposal, drawing, or your portfolio. Once a

task is completed, destroy the reminder so your bulletin board stays current.

Additionally, you'll need a computer, printer, and basic office supplies (envelopes, paper, paper clips, stamps, pads, pencils, and so on).

MONEY SAVERS: Office supplies, especially paper, can be expensive. Save money by investigating local discount office supply stores. Warehouse stores such as Office Depot, OfficeMax, and Staples feature huge inventories of heavily discounted office equipment. They buy in volume and pass on hefty savings to customers.

4. *Buy secondhand.* If you are considering buying a new computer or printer, investigate secondhand sources. Don't argue that you don't want anybody's headache or lemon. Buying office equipment is not like buying a car. First, new equipment is very expensive. Second, many people, especially small entrepreneurs, upgrade their equipment yearly. Yes, technology changes monthly. But it doesn't change radically. This year's equipment should be good for at least 5 years. Third, and most important, secondhand equipment is dramatically cheaper than new models, often by more than 50 percent.

ADVICE

Scan publications like *Buy Lines* and ads in daily newspapers advertising secondhand office equipment. A couple of years ago, I picked up a secondhand fax machine for $75. It's hard to beat a bargain like that. And, yes, it's still working. *Caution:* Also know you are taking your chances. Sometimes you get what you pay for. It's worth the risk.

Now, we're cooking. Your job-hunting command center is ready, so prepare to organize your day.

Make Time Count by Structuring Your Day

Everything is in place, you're dressed and ready to go to work, so make the time count. How you do so is up to you. I'm going to pass on some suggestions. Consider it a blueprint that can be improved as your job hunt progresses.

ADVICE

Few mortals bound out of bed ready to go. Plan your day the night before so you can start your day focused and motivated. For example, write down the names of companies you want to research and people you hope to reach.

However you plan your time, the goal is to be ready to jump on hot leads when they surface. If you don't, someone else will. Remember, you've got plenty of competition. *Fact:* Harvard economist James Medoff reported that the number of job openings available to a job searcher has dropped 37 percent since 1984. It's yet another reminder that the job market is more competitive than ever.

Consider this sample schedule.

Morning

6:00 a.m.–7:30 a.m. After you're fueled by a half-dozen cups of coffee, pore over the newspaper. Start with the want ads. They are a long shot, but they're still worth scanning. You can't afford not to run down every possible avenue. Then scan the business pages for leads (corporate acquisitions, start-up companies, and more).

7:30 a.m.–8:30 a.m. Wind up business started the day before. Finish letters, complete research, and return calls.

8:30 a.m.–12:00 p.m. By 10:30 a.m., you should be preparing to hit the field to go on information interviews or to follow up leads. Ideally, half the morning should be spent in your office, the rest in the field.

Afternoon

12:00 p.m.–2:00 p.m. The lunch period is the worst time to call people, yet it is an ideal time for information gathering at libraries and trade organizations. Unless lunch is related to job hunting or is part of a job interview, don't waste too much time on it. Spend 15 minutes to inhale a sandwich and coffee. Any more than that and you're wasting precious time.

2:00 p.m.–3:30 p.m. Don't lose steam. Pick up where you left off. Meet people, gather information, and schedule job interviews.

3:30 p.m.–6:00 p.m. Try to spend the remaining part of the day in your office doing paperwork, mailing letters, and returning phone calls. Hopefully, you'll be greeted by a bunch of messages. Now is the time to corner busy people. As the day winds down, people will be more inclined to schmooze with you on the phone.

Take a break. It's not always possible, but from time to time, try to take a 30- to 45-minute exercise break. Get out of the house for a jog, run, bike ride, and so on. You'll release pent-up energy and return to your office charged and invigorated.

Evening

7:00 p.m.–8:30 p.m. No, your day isn't over yet. But you're almost there. Now that you've digested your dinner, this is an excellent time to plan the next day and do some quiet reflecting before you turn off your desk lamp and call it a night.

It's a rough schedule, but that's what fruitful job hunting is all about. Like I said, job searching ought to be a full-time job in itself. There are few accidents or lucky breaks in life. The more involved you become in the job quest, the faster you'll see results.

POSITIVE SIGN: If you're wiped out and can't wait to crawl into bed at the end of a long day of job hunting, you know you're doing a good job. Believe it or not, that's a hell of a good feeling.

Priceless Tips on Connecting with Busy People

Face-to-face contact is the best way to make a lasting impression. But before you can sit down with prospective employers and impress them, you're going to have to log in countless hours finding the appropriate decision makers and scheduling appointments. Your biggest allies are secretaries and assistants. They are the gatekeepers. If you're dumb enough to irritate them with a nasty attitude, you'll never secure an appointment.

The Telephone Ought to Be Your Best Friend

Meanwhile, it wouldn't hurt to polish your phone skills so the device becomes an extension of your body. If you've got a problem using the phone—you're shy, uptight, self-conscious—confront your fears and get over them. If you don't, you'll miss out on opportunities. Realize that a negative phone persona puts people off. The person on the other end doesn't say to himself or herself, "This person has a hang-up so I better be understanding." Rather, the reaction is, "What's with this guy's tone? Who does he think he is?" The other person doesn't hear a problem, but assumes you have a nasty attitude.

It doesn't take a shrink to overcome phone phobia either. Just practice. Start by understanding that no one likes the sound of his or her own voice. It's practically a genetic trait.

Buy an inexpensive telephone microphone and start taping your conversations. Rather than just taping job-related calls, record all your conversations so you can hear the difference between business and social calls. Typically, people with phone hang-ups get uptight when they deem one conversation more important than another. They'll be relaxed and casual when speaking to their spouses, friends, or mothers, but then become uptight and breathy when talking to potential employers.

Goal: Find a middle ground by striking a balance between the two tones.

Listen closely to each voice. Write down the differences and how you'd correct them. The best way to establish a relaxed, yet professional vocal tone is by preparing yourself. Phone hang-ups stem from a fear of rejection. Lick the problem by making a list of worst-case scenarios. For example, the voice on the other end:

- Slams the phone down in your face
- Brutally interrogates you
- Asks embarrassing or off-putting questions
- Seems impatient, preoccupied, short, belligerent
- Tells you to take a hike

You get the idea. Look at each of these scenarios and prepare a defense. The more thought you give to each, the easier it will be to have a professional comeback. Before you jot down a comeback, here's a bit of lifesaving advice. The critical mistake made by most phone hang-up sufferers is taking rejection personally. Ponder that for a minute. You hear a nasty voice and you immediately think: "This woman has it in for me. She hates skinny, dark-haired men from Brooklyn." Does that sound nuts? You bet it is. Maybe I exaggerated, but paranoia is very common. The person on the other end of the phone will react to your voice, and may even form a mental image of you. Otherwise, you're only a voice—pleasant, interesting, or dull. Unless this person has clapped eyes on you, there is nothing else to go on.

The only way to respond to *any* voice, whether curt or polite, is by sounding professional. Tell yourself that most introductory phone conversations are brief and superficial. More often than not, you're asking either for information or for an appointment. If the person can't help out, the conversation ends. It's only later, when you're actually being considered for a job and are in the interview hot seat, that real pressure is applied and tough questions are hurled at you. Until then, concentrate on the preliminary details. A good phone personality is one of the most critical.

Test for Upgrading Your Phone Persona

Even if you don't have a phone hang-up, it doesn't hurt to improve your telephone persona. A quick way is by taking this telephone rapport questionnaire:

1. Is your voice audible and your tone consistent?
2. Do you use clear, simple, declarative sentences?
3. Do you slur words?
4. Does a regional accent get in your way?
5. What can you do to change, correct, or improve your voice?

No cheating. If you answered no to the first four questions and "nothing" to the fifth, you're a veritable telephone superstar. But that's hard to believe. If you're honest with yourself, chances are you could stand to bone up on one or two of the above items.

Let's move on and get our computer act together.

CHAPTER 8

WELCOME TO CYBERSPACE

RULE 8 You had better be computer-literate, or you'll never work in this town again.

Don't tell me you don't know any of these terms: *RAM, byte, input, modem,* or *the Internet.* If you think it sounds like gobbledygook, keep this to yourself. Not only is it uncool to admit you know nothing about computers, it's downright dumb. You might as well be living in the hinterlands of Appalachia. You can't expect to job-hunt successfully in the global 1990s without technological know-how.

If no part of this sermon applies to you, jump to the next chapter. My feelings won't be hurt. But if you are one of the many who get nervous at the very mention of the word *computers,* I urge you to read every word. This is a serious issue. Knowing next to nothing about computers seriously hinders any job search. Your marketability instantly plummets. *Fact:* You wouldn't be wrong assuming *all* employers want someone with basic computer skills. That means familiarity with DOS Windows or Macintosh systems.

Not knowing how to take advantage of readily available software also mars your research capabilities. You'll be restricted to conventional print sources and miss out on a smorgasbord of on-line databases.

Aside from the practical and competitive reasons for understanding technology, taking advantage of technological bells and whistles is fun. It may seem daunting to the uninitiated, but *once* you are bitten by the technological bug, I guarantee you'll be hooked forever.

Before you know it, you'll be tapping into bulletin boards and communicating via modem.

Getting Up to Speed

Don't be embarrassed if you're computer-phobic. You're not alone. Some corporate executives who earn six-figure salaries are also terrified of computers. Rather than wallow in indifference, apathy, or ignorance, do something about it.

If you're seriously agoraphobic, an incorrigible kleptomaniac, or an obsessive eater, you would find a good psychological program or a reasonably priced shrink to handle it. Similarly, if you don't know the first thing about computers, tap the endless information sources that tell you more than you need to know.

The good news is it's easy to get up to speed. The wonderful phrase that will lower your anxiety level a few notches is *user-friendly*. That's the catchall term people like to hear and, for obvious reasons, a term that computer firms market to the hilt. Simply, it means you don't have to be a computer programmer or systems engineer to learn how to use a computer. Most of the software out there is simple enough for a child to use. Even chimpanzees have been trained to perform simple computer tasks, so don't tell me you can't learn.

Before you pop into your nearest computer store, check out your friends' equipment. Ask them to give you a demonstration and then start playing with the keyboard and mouse. Browse through computer stores to familiarize yourself with models and prices. Get to know the salespeople and ask questions. With each step you're learning more. After 3 weeks of shopping around and becoming familiar with DOS and Apple products, you'll be at a critical juncture. Since your fear has dissipated, maybe even disappeared, you can take one of two routes: You have enough information to buy a system or take a computer course teaching basic software programs. I urge the former approach. The reason is that once you know what you want and you've tested several systems, you're fully capable of teaching yourself everything you need to know. If I can do it—I'm not ashamed to admit I was terrified of the mysterious machines until I bought my first computer in 1985—you can also. Again, don't forget those precious words: *user-friendly.*

Only a decade ago, computers and accompanying software were pretty complicated. You had to spend hours poring over manuals before you could even turn on your computer. Then, it took a week before you were actually up and running. Today, many computers come fully loaded. That means they have all the software you need. All you have to do is turn on the computer on and go to work. And, with easy-to-use Windows software, you don't even have to memorize commands. So you see, the computer companies are not kidding when they say their equipment is easy to use. It doesn't take a rocket scientist to know that the best way to sell computers is by making them so simple dummies like us don't suffer anxiety attacks before we try to use them. I guarantee you'll be pleasantly surprised when you discover how simple many systems are. You'll say to yourself, "Where have I been? This stuff is incredible!"

Master the Lingo

Once you've mastered your computer, you're ready to explore cyberspace and check out the Internet. The Internet is a global network of computer information databases. While the Internet is the technology topic of the day, it actually took shape more than a decade ago. It's estimated that the network links more than 2.2 million computers on some 33,000 networks and is accessible in 135 countries. Reportedly, 25 million people can send electronic mail messages on the Internet. It's no wonder the business world is aggressively taking advantage of the Internet. It's impossible to even estimate the number of commercial computers involved in the process of linking directly to the Internet. Each month, dozens of companies are advertising their products and services on the Internet. One source estimated that the Internet represents a $10-billion-a-year business. Whether this estimate is accurate or not, the Internet is a powerful communications tool that can't be ignored. It is global in scope and never shuts down.

No passing fad, the Net will be the research tool of the future. If you doubt its importance, the Associated Press, a traditional news organization formed in the middle of the nineteenth century, stepped into the twenty-first century in 1995 when it announced it would distribute its articles and photographs over the global Internet. A *New York Times* reporter deemed it a significant turning point, saying, "It was simply the latest, but perhaps most historically significant, move by an old-line media organization onto the World Wide Web, the Internet multimedia information-retrieval system that appears on the verge of becoming a mass medium itself."

Internet Hot Spots: Check Out Home Page Help Wanteds

Take the hint and become a Net surfer. I'm not talking about a newfangled sport. Net surfing is technospeak for sprinting around the Internet. Learning how to net surf masterfully can be a valuable job-hunting skill.

Companies are wising up. They're bypassing employment agencies and headhunters and casting for candidates on their own World Wide Web "home pages." Simply, it means companies have found a neat, inexpensive way to find bodies that eliminates paying hefty fees for headhunters and running classified ads in daily newspapers. Here's how it works. As hundreds of companies are jumping onto the Net, many are searching for candidates on their World Wide Web home pages. *U.S. News & World Report* reported, "With the number of home pages exploding, the Web is becoming a must-see for job hunters." Typically, a home page carries more information than the bare-bones job descriptions found in newspapers and trade magazines. The home pages also provide important information about the company, such as mission statement, product descriptions, employee benefits, and press releases about current news. It's a great way to get a snapshot of the company so you can prepare for an interview. Home pages are easy to access and are designed to be consumer friendly. In fact, some Web sites have a mechanism that allows job hunters to search openings by occupation or desired geographic location.

On-line entrepreneurs insist that classified listings on the Internet will replace traditional print classified ads. I doubt that will happen. Nevertheless, you're foolish not to check out on-line job listings. Each year, more companies are offering them. Career Mosaic (www.careermosaic.com), which is operated by Bernard Hodes Advertising in New York, boasts one of the largest classified Web sites, with more than 23,000 job listings. Well over 200 companies use it to post job listings and approximately 400,000 job searchers are following up on the listings. Like the home page, electronic classifieds offer snappy graphics as well as audio and video clips, color photographs, and other features not found in traditional newspaper listings. Through Career Mosaic, job hunters can fill out on-line employment applications. Some companies offer elaborate descriptions of their corporate culture and values.

Newspapers also have jumped on the Internet. Going beyond on-line classifieds, six of the largest newspapers, including *The New York Times*, the *Washington Post*, and the *Los Angeles Times*, banded together to form an on-line job listing service. More newspapers from other major markets are planning to join the service. It's not hard to figure out why they're doing it either. As one newspaper executive put it, "He who has the biggest database will make the marketplace."

If you want to learn more about job hunting on the Internet, here are three books that can help you out: *Hook Up, Get Hired! The Internet Job Revolution* by Joyce Laine Kennedy (John Wiley & Sons), *Be Your Own Headhunter On-line* by Pam Dixon and Sylvia Tiersten (Random House), and *The On-Line Job Search Companion* by James C. Gonyea (McGraw-Hill).

Check Out On-Line Services

Once you've become an ace net surfer, check out on-line job-searching avenues. In the last 2 years, several national on-line employment advertising services have surfaced. Many of them allow job hunters to search through listings of more than 5000 openings. You can also list your qualifications in their databanks. Many on-line services charge a modest fee; some are free. Some commercial on-line services are also offering specialized bulletin boards, allowing job searchers to post their résumés via electronic mail and respond to job announcements.

Take the economical route first. Before checking out commercial on-line job-hunting services, investigate the freebies. Most states provide job banks through more than 2000 employment services throughout the United States. State governments are unwieldy bureaucracies, but they're also a wealth of career information. If you didn't know it, every state is federally funded to operate a labor exchange or employment service free to employers and job applicants. Most states also offer on-line job listings. You just sit in front of a personal computer and look for jobs of interest by moving through a series of occupational categories. Check your telephone book for a list of the nearest state employment office.

If your state employment office has nothing that interests you, look into the following commercial on-line services

America Online, Inc. (8619 Westwood Center Drive, Vienna, VA 22182). AOL offers databases for job searchers and entrepreneurs. Its Career Center database contains 4000 jobs throughout the United States, is accessible 24 hours a day, and is updated weekly. Creator Jim Gonyea insists it's the fist electronic career guidance and employment center in the country. True or not, the on-line service offers great information. The Occupational Profiles database, for example, details more than 700 occupations, along with information about specific companies, working conditions, job outlooks, and salary ranges.

CompuServe Information Service (P.O. Box 20212, Columbus, OH 43220). A popular offering is its on-line headhunting service, which amounts to a fast and cheap way to find bodies without contending with employment agencies or executive recruiters.

Your qualifications are accessible on-line to hundreds of Fortune 500 companies and start-up companies. If a sharp-eyed human resources person thinks you match a job description, you'll be called in for an interview. CompuServe says 100 new companies log on each week.

Peterson's Guides (P.O. Box 2123, Carnegie Center, Princeton, NJ 08543). If you didn't know it, the entrepreneurial folks publishing college guides and career books also offer the on-line service called Connexion, which is pretty much a variation of the above. Applicants' qualifications are made available to more than 200 companies and executive recruiters across the United States.

Play All Cards

Technology is great, but don't put all your eggs in one basket. It's fun, not to mention very *now,* to travel the information highway for job leads. It adds a whole new dimension to job hunting. While you're certainly exploiting cutting-edge technology, don't mistakenly think all the information is exclusive. Job searchers have complained that many job listings are out of date and many have already been filled. America Online's Jim Gonyea admitted that many of his job listings appeared as paid ads elsewhere. His service rewrote the ads and posted them. It doesn't sound legal, but copyright attorneys say the practice is acceptable as long as the on-line services don't use the same language as the original ad.

And listing applications on-line doesn't mean prospective employers will read them.

Put it all together and see on-line services as nothing more than another job source. Don't expect fantastic results. Right now, it's new and exciting, and thus surrounded by hype. A few years from now, I'm betting on-line services will be compared with newspaper want ads because the odds of getting interviews will be so high.

As for exploring cyberspace, stay tuned because the best is yet to come. Right now, it represents a vast and unregulated frontier everyone is trying to explore. It's no wonder there is a glut of services. But that's about to change, as a shake-up is projected over the next few years. Many of the services will fall by the wayside, with stronger ones taking their place.

Let's rock on and bone up on corporate-speak.

CHAPTER 9

CORPORATE-SPEAK APPLICANTS ONLY!

RULE 9 Employers demand that applicants be fluent in conversational "corporate-speak."

"You say you just speak English? Sorry, Ms. Flugger. We're interviewing only bilingual applicants."

"How can that be? You're an American company with no overseas divisions. What language skills are you looking for?"

"Get with the program, Ms. Flugger. We need folks who speak fluent 'corporate-speak' as well. Sorry."

Sound bizarre? The above fictional tale carries a powerful message: Companies want applicants who cannot only walk the walk, but talk the talk. That means more than mastering the King's English. It also means being conversant in the corporate patois called organizational- or corporate-speak.

Remember how everyone in the George Orwell classic *1984* was ordered to speak the official government-sanctioned language called "Newspeak"? If you didn't speak it, you were shipped off to some remote gulag to spend your days smashing rocks and drinking frozen borscht.

Thankfully, we don't live in a totalitarian dictatorship where you're required to speak a government-approved lingo. And it does not mean companies won't hire you if you aren't fluent in corporate-speak. But if you can, you'll be better off while getting a leg up on your competition. Once hired, don't expect to ascend the corporate ladder unless you pick up on this language skill.

Don't tell me you don't have a clue what corporate-speak is. Simply, it's English spiced with corporate buzzwords that have no meaning outside of the organization. If you're going to speak it, you had better know which buzzwords are hot and which are on their way out. Drop the wrong buzzword to the wrong person at the wrong time and you've signed your death warrant. Suddenly, you're branded out of touch, a throwback to a primitive corporate era. You're weakening your position, sowing the seeds for your destruction.

Don't despair. You don't have to call Berlitz for a course in corporate-speak. There's a much cheaper route. I heartily recommend the bible of buzzwords, Charles B. Wendel and Elaine Svensson's *Business Buzzwords: Everything You Need to Know to Speak the Lingo of the 90s* (Amacom). The book includes popular buzzwords such as *reengineering, downsizing, teamnets, TQM, balanced scorecard, learning organization,* and *gain-sharing*. Say the authors:

> In a culture where we prefer sound bytes to in-depth commentary, have an attention span molded by the 15-second commercial, and consider music videos art, business buzzwords are the ideal communication tool for recasting our imagery of the corporate world. Packaging the visual impact of computer graphics with the intellectual content of a special-purpose lexicon, words and phrases such as horizontal management, rightsizing, mass-customization, and paradigm shift provide an intelligent interpretation of rapidly shifting market realities.

The authors go on to explain buzzwords' importance. The Information Age, they say, demands a shorthand "across the electronic networks linking the new corporation." Buzzwords facilitate that communications stream, offering a communications code understandable to its players.

Buzzwords go part and parcel with our supersonic global culture. They can be likened to hit songs or this year's fashions. What you see on Parisian and American runways one year will be passé the next. It's pretty much the same with business buzzwords. They have a short lifespan, forcing corporate fast trackers to be au courant.

The key to staying on top of buzzwords is knowing their creators. Since buzzwords have a short life, today's reigning gurus will be dethroned a couple of years down the road.

Meet the Buzzword Gurus

By the same token, don't take all this buzzword stuff too seriously. If you do, you're in big trouble. Since the buzzword creators take themselves *very* seriously, it's all the more reason that you must approach it with a sense of humor. Strip away their intellectual pretense and you have smooth-talking word hucksters dispensing management philosophy with a unique language accompanying it.

Nevertheless, they're a fascinating bunch. Depending on your perspective, they're a cross between snake oil charmers, cult leaders, MBA-toting tin men, and brilliant business tacticians. They include college professors, high-paid management consultants, economists, and academic writers. Many of the superstars, such as Tom Peters and Robert Waterman, boast incredible credentials. Before Peters and Waterman began pulling down hefty consulting fees, they worked for prestigious blue-chip consulting firm McKinsey & Company. A few years of service in a high-profile consulting firm is an immediate career catapult.

The best of these trendsetters milk the speaking circuit for all it's worth, pulling down sickening fees lecturing to businesspeople and students. Reportedly, Peters, the high priest of business consultants, makes (are you ready?) $60,000 for less than 2 hours on the podium. Staggering, right?

Practically all the superstar buzzword creators have books to their name. Peters, for example, boasts a string of high-grossers that include *In Search of Excellence, Thriving on Chaos,* and *Liberation*

Management: Necessary Disorganization for the Nanosecond Nineties.

Whatever their backgrounds or credentials, they're all clever entrepreneurs with an uncanny knack for self-promotion. It's no wonder people listen to them and big-name corporations pay them outrageously high consulting fees to overhaul their organizations.

Knowing that buzzwords are the flesh and blood of corporate-speak, you'd best become familiar with their creators. Again, I refer you to Wendel and Svensson's *Business Buzzwords.* A few of the leaders profiled by the authors are Warren Bennis, Philip Crosby, Edward de Bono, Gary Hamel and C.K. Prahalad, Michael Hammer and James Champy, Charles Handy, Rosabeth Moss Kanter, David Nadler, Kenichi Ohmae, Tom Peters, Michael Porter, Frederick Reichheld, Charles Savage, Peter Senge, George Stalk, Robert M. Tomasko, and Robert Waterman. They also include the buzzwords that made them famous. Ready for a test? Who coined the expressions *informed optimism* and *positive attitudes and attention exhibited by management?* If you said Robert Waterman, you're right. And what about *bucky-borgs, deorganized,* and *disembodied enterprise?* Tom Peters is the correct answer.

ADVICE

To stay on top of this gobbledygook doesn't mean you have to drop a bundle on their books. Instead, religiously follow reliable business rags such as *Fortune, Forbes, Entrepreneur, Inc., Business Week,* and *Nation's Business,* and you'll always be up to speed.

Want to stay ahead of the pack? *Business Buzzwords* also tells you how to create a buzzword. You'll be pleasantly shocked to discover it is a simple process of selecting, at most, three words. You just choose that word that describes the "where," focus on the "how," and name "what" will be affected by this management theory. Do you think you can come up with next year's rightsizing, TQM, process reengineering, or PRG (performance-related gift)? Come up with some fancy terms no one understands, fabricate a convoluted philosophy, package them together, and then take the whole shebang on the road. If you make a pile of money, send me a commission for giving you the idea.

But if you're like most working stiffs, concentrate instead on staying fluent in the trendy buzzwords of the hour. More than being a hit at cocktail parties, you will be primed and ready to impress the pants (or skirt) off any prospective employer.

Here are a few fast-track buzzwords you had better know if you hope to wheel-and-deal in the twenty-first century.

Cross-functional. Multifaceted 1990s workers who can thrive in a downsized company by performing many tasks well. Simply, jacks-of-all-trades and masters of all.

Electronic sweatshop. A high-tech workspace in which managers use technology to monitor your productivity. That's right, Big Brother is watching you.

Mouse potato. Couch potatoes are passé. They've been replaced by the 1990s version of the computer nerd. And they've gained respectability too. The computer is more than a necessity for these techies; it's practically an extension of their bodies.

Netspeak. The official language of the Internet, what else?

Open-collar worker. Blue-collar and white-collar workers are rapidly going the way of the dinosaur. The 1990s telecommuters are called open-collar workers because they don't have to "dress for success." In fact, they don't have to dress at all. They can work stark naked in front of their computer monitors and not have to clap eyes on another human being for months—maybe years.

Spamming. The Internet equivalent of junk mail. It happens through the random cluttering of cyberspace with advertising, sales, or promotional messages no one wants to read.

Vertical disintegration. A system by which companies replace full-time workers with contract workers. Take the concept to its logical conclusion and you have the ultimate virtual organization: a company of one. No kidding.

Webmaster. Meet the archetypal middle manager. These are the folks who will be managing one of the 100,000 sites on the Internet's World Wide Web.

Might as Well Bone Up on Doublespeak Too

Now that you're into deciphering strange tongues, why not go the extra mile and learn doublespeak as well? I'm not putting you on. You've heard the term and I'm sure you've heard plenty of doublespeak in your day. The frightening part is you didn't know it was doublespeak—all the more reason you ought to bring yourself up to speed. Where corporate-speak communicates through descriptive buzzwords, doublespeak is designed to distort meaning and confuse the hell out of listeners and readers.

Example: Your boss calls you into her office, closes the door, and says, "Timmy, we're restructuring in order to position ourselves for greater future growth." You'd feel like a real jerk if you got excited and said you wanted to be part of the team spearheading the company's growth. If you translated the confusing string of words, you'd know you were being axed. That's right, empty your desk, you've been dejobbed (that's another hot doublespeak word).

I bet you're wondering why companies don't put their cards on the table and simply say what they mean. The answer is they work hard at creating the illusion that they're altruistic rather than cold, money-making machines. Remember, this is the age of the humanistic company in which bosses are supposed to be sympathetic people who empower their workers, encourage diversity, and respect affirmative action. Perish the thought they should just be themselves—profit-starved entrepreneurs guarding their bottom lines. If they ran the company like they were playing a heated game of Monopoly, there wouldn't be any need for doublespeak.

Instead, companies hire talented word crafters to create doublespeak. Workers aren't laid off or fired any more; they're surplussed, destaffed, released, dehired, selected out, or nonretained. Companies aren't getting smaller; they're rightsizing or eliminating redundancies in their human resources pool. When Chrysler bought out American Motors, the giant automaker laid off lots of people. But instead of telling it like it is, company spin doctors came up with some classy doublespeak to describe the event: "Career enhancement alternative program." Do you think that made the thousands of people handed pink slips feel better?

In early 1992, Bank of America announced it was about to conduct a "release of resources." You guessed it: The giant bank laid off 14,000 workers. Here's three more popular terms for firing used by big companies: *enhance the efficiency of operations, rationalization of marketing efforts,* and *take appropriate cost-reduction actions.* You get the idea.

It's obvious why you ought to know when doublespeak is being hurled at you. First, it raises your sophistication level to a higher plateau. Second, and more important, no one will mess with your head by sidestepping the truth in an indirect or underhanded way.

Doublespeak is "language that pretends to communicate but really doesn't," according William Lutz, author of *Doublespeak* (HarperCollins). Lutz is a professor of English at Rutgers University and chairman of the Committee on Public Doublespeak of the National Council of Teachers. He also edits the *Quarterly Review of Doublespeak.* I strongly suggest you read Lutz's book and subscribe to his newsletter (National Council of Teachers of English, 1111 West Kenyon Road, Urbana, IL 61801-1096). I guarantee no one will ever get away with doublespeaking at you again. Doublespeak "conceals or prevents thought rather than extending thought," says

Lutz. At its worst, it eliminates thought altogether. Liken it to doublethink, as described in *1984*. ("The mental process that allows you to hold two opposing ideas in your mind at the same time and believe in both of them.") Lutz says doublespeak "enables speaker and listener, writer and reader, to hold two opposing ideas in their minds at the same time and believe in both of them. At its least offensive, doublespeak is inflated language that tries to give importance to the insignificant."

Lutz will tell you everything you've ever wanted to know about doublespeak. Contrary to popular belief, it's not a product of the 1990s. Actually, it's been around for centuries. Julius Caesar, for one, was a master at it. In his account of the Gallic Wars, Caesar described his brutal and bloody conquest and subjugation of Gaul as "pacifying Gaul." He goes on to say that when traitors were put to death in Rome, the announcement of their execution was made in the form of saying "they have lived." And "taking notice of a man in the ancestral manner" meant capital punishment. "The prisoner was then led away" meant he was executed.

That's just a taste. Here are some definitions of commonly used doublespeak terms from Lutz's book.

Doublespeak	*Translation*
1. Single use	Disposable
2. Safety-related occurrence	Accident
3. Environmentally stabilized	Polluted
4. Initiate a proactive action	Recall defective product
5. Fourth-quarter equity retreat	Stock market crash
6. Environmental technician	Janitor
7. Unauthorized withdrawal	Bank robbery
8. Strategic misrepresentation	Lie
9. Price enhancement	Higher prices
10. Value-oriented retailing	Discounting
11. Advisory marketing representative	Salesperson
12. Sales plan was too aggressive	Business is bad
13. Marketing consultant	Salesperson

14.	Nonperforming assets	Bad loans
15.	Renewed appliance	Used refrigerator
16.	Invest in	Buy or spend
17.	Volume variances from plan	Strikes
18.	Automotive internist	Car mechanic

If this discussion has made you mad, you're experiencing the right emotion. You should be angry. Most doublespeak is designed to dupe and confuse. In fact, we seldom even question it. But, not any more.

ADVICE

Don't accept doublespeak. Question and challenge it. If you don't know what something means, ask for a definition. Keep on doing so until people communicate in plain English. Not only will it keep you sharp, but no one will try to verbally trick you again.

What's more, speaking plain English is the only way to be a straight-ahead networker, which we're going to get into now.

CHAPTER 10

YOU CALL THAT NETWORKING!

RULE 10 Olympic-class networkers get the *best* jobs.

Everyone I know is networking. If my turtle could talk, he'd tell me he's networking too. What's all the fuss about? The answer is networking is a euphemism for politically correct job searching. The result is that millions of words have been expended on the subject, not to mention the half-dozen or more books published on networking.

The thinking goes like this: If you're not networking, you're spinning wheels and wasting precious time. It sounds silly, but this statement holds more than a grain of truth. Conventional wisdom says masterful networkers not only find out about job leads faster than most people, but they are also in the most strategic position to leap on opportunities. The wheeler-dealers and decision makers of the world are relentless Olympic-style networkers.

They're in the minority, however. Ninety percent of the people who swear they're networking are going about it in the wrong way.

Let's clear the deck, go back to basics, and find out what *real* networking is all about.

What Is Networking Anyway?

Networking's origins date back to the beginning of civilization. Adam was the first networker. Networking starts when people realize they need one another's help. It's not just for job getting, but for everything from mating and hunting to conquering the wilds. In short, networking is more than a social tool; it is also a survival mechanism.

However, the pursuit remained nameless until the mid-1970s, when working women formed support groups, which they dubbed networks, to help one another secure jobs and to provide career guidance. Ideally, a high-functioning network consisted of an elaborate chain of contacts threading through virtually every crevice of an industry. Once career gurus endorsed and christened the concept, it wasn't long before networking was widely touted as a crucial career-building technique.

While the definition makes sense and the theory behind networking is indisputable, most job hunters have formed self-styled networking techniques, most of which yield meager results. The reasons tell the whole story.

Bad Networking/Good Networking

I'm not going to insult you by saying you ought to be networking. You already know that. In some form or fashion, you've been doing it throughout your career. But I am going to take you to the next level, passing along secrets and insights you may not have considered.

First, a true story about a buddy who swears he's a dynamite networker. Each time he loses a job, which is about every 3 or 4 years, he turns his networking machine to full throttle and becomes a whirling dervish. But no one ever told him he isn't going anywhere. The results of his efforts are usually dismal, to say the least. First, he blankets the universe with his résumé and business cards, sending them to everyone he knows, remotely knows, or presumes to know, plus friends of friends, contacts of contacts, you name it. If he thought he had some remote link to the Pope, he'd send him a résumé too. The man spares no expense in getting out the word. Naturally, each résumé is accompanied by a short cover letter, which briefly introduces him, whetting the reader's appetite for the résumé behind it. Thanks to his computer and high-speed printer, he's able to turn out these letters en masse by simply changing the name, address, and date on each.

The cover letter says he's the greatest worker in the galaxy and is looking for new employment opportunities to challenge his superior intellect and capabilities. (My friend swears the world is waiting for him.)

He also goes to untold lengths to try to meet with potential contacts face-to-face. Countless hours are invested going to networking parties. It doesn't matter what kind they are either—chamber of commerce, church or synagogue groups, YMCA, the weekly meeting of Widget Grinders Anonymous, you name it. Call this person a nonsectarian, nondenominational networker. If he thought it would be worth his while handing out his résumé at cocktail parties for neurosurgeons or paleontologists, he'd be there, business cards in hand, flashing his million-dollar smile.

When not involved in the above activities, he's constantly on the phone following up on his mass mailings and checking in with the people he meets at networking parties. When he's not making follow-up calls, he's cold-calling people he hardly knows. If he thinks someone can help him, he'll put in a call. A typical phone conversation sounds something like this: "Is this Ted Ogelbottom? This is Barney Fullthrottle and I'm calling to say how ya doing and to let ya know I'm in the throes of looking for a new position as a cyberspace copywriter. I hope you received the résumé and cover letter I sent you. You haven't? Well, that's too bad, Mr. Ogelbottom. It must be in the mail. You know how backed up it gets around holiday time. Would you mind if I send you another and call you back to discuss potential opportunities at Cyberspace Ltd.? I have more than 100 years of experience in the field and I know I can be an asset to your company....I look forward to speaking with you soon, Mr. Ogelbottom."

The man is tireless. He'll make at least 30 calls a day and get absolutely nowhere. If he's lucky, someone will actually take pity on him and ask him to come in for an interview. It doesn't take much gray matter to see that this poor guy is spitting in the proverbial wind. Suffice it to say, he's doing everything wrong.

You can also guess what the reaction is to his calls. If you were running a company, how would you react if you got a call from Barney Fullthrottle? If you're mean-spirited, you might even hang up the phone on him while he's in the middle of his spiel. More realistically, you'll be polite, thank him for considering your company, tell him you'll look at the résumé, and call if there is any interest in him. If you're superpolite, you'll have your assistant send off a thanks-but-no-thanks note.

The overall reaction will be something like "Is this guy for real?" No matter what scenario you choose, Fullthrottle strikes out.

I've tried to help, but he won't listen. Sooner or later, he's bound to get the message. Meanwhile, he's wasting precious time.

Take the hint and don't make the same mistakes. If I've hit some responsive chords, don't make a mad dash for the nearest open window. Just abort what you've been doing and start fresh. It's never too late to learn.

Three Networking No-Nos

Mind these three networking no-nos and you'll be off to a good start.

1. *Randomly calling anyone.* Buckshot approaches don't work. They violate all the rules of good networking. The smart person neither makes assumptions about nor underestimates other people. This fact of life is ingrained in accomplished networkers, who conscientiously build their networks the way the Egyptians built their pyramids. They start by building an impenetrable foundation of people they know and with whom they have a rapport. From there, they build their network by slowly, yet persistently adding new people. The key word is *connection.* Good networking is all about building strong connections.

ADVICE

Accomplished networkers have a sixth sense about people. They don't waste time randomly calling anyone who crosses their path. They confine their calls to people they've met or people who were recommended by a reliable contact. And they have the discretion to call at appropriate times when they can capture the person's undivided attention. For example, the best time to call high-stressed fast-trackers is late in the day, preferably after 5 p.m. This is when the drones flee and the brass start cleaning up their desks and getting things done.

2. *Contacting people you haven't spoken to in a long time.* How do you feel about being hit up for a favor from someone you haven't spoken to in 10 years? All of a sudden you get a call that goes something like this: "Ted, I bet you'll never guess who this is? Give up? It's Arnie Klopperpest. Remember? We worked together at Bundrally Cannons on the Dammstadt account designing pocket-sized hand grenades. How ya been? It's got to be at least 8 years since we spoke to each other. I thought we might get together for a drink to discuss old times, and I'd like to get your input on some possible job leads. I've been out of work for about 7 months and I'm looking for a new programming position. I thought you might have some suggestions. What's your schedule like? How about this Thursday, June 10, at 6:30 p.m. at O'Reilly's Bar? I'll even buy the first round." You get the idea.

I don't know how you would react, but I know what my reaction would be. As Arnie rambles on, I'd be trying to find a creative way to get this guy off my back. Talk about being presumptuous. Eight years go by and all of a sudden he pops up with the chutzpah to ask for job leads. Offering to buy a round of drinks is certainly no inducement for getting together. Even if we did get together, there would be no incentive to help him. Nobody likes fair-weather opportunistic friends. This is offensive networking.

Real networkers stay in touch and are not lazy about it either. That doesn't mean calling every person in your network every week. Many career networkers have networks consisting of 200 to 300 people.

ADVICE

As a general rule, speak to everyone in your network every 6 months. Needless to say, there will be powerful and influential contacts you'll want to speak to on a weekly or biweekly basis. The idea is to stay in touch. And you don't have to have any reason for calling other than to find out how the other person is doing. That's right. No motive or agenda. You're just calling to shoot the breeze. That's real networking. It elevates the people-cultivating game to an art.

REMEMBER: A strong, resilient network is made up of well-defined relationships cultivated over time. Like they say, there is no such thing as fast friends. Seasoned networkers never ask favors of people with whom they have no relationship. That's just bad form.

George C. Fraser, publisher of *SuccessGuide,* a guide to African-American career resources, says, "Networking is all about building a universe of people who can help you. It is meeting and sharing mutual opportunities with like-minded businesspeople in a casual and less-than-formal setting." The heart and soul of great networking, asserts Fraser, is building an "infrastructure of support."

3. *Intrusive or inappropriately aggressive behavior.* Real networkers employ tact and diplomacy. They have a nose for potential contacts, an ability to read the landscape to know when to make their move. You're not going learn these traits in school. But you are going to learn them on the street talking to people and developing potential contacts. Through constant practice, you'll get to the point where you have instincts about people. Your gut will tell you when to advance, pull back, lay low, or abort.

   Amateur networkers, on the other hand, stand out from the crowd. The worst display a sense of entitlement. They think the world owes them a living. Making matters worse, many have a bad attitude. If they can't read people and have a distorted sense of the world, it's no wonder they're always putting both feet in their mouths and making fools of themselves. Like Arnie Klopperpest, they'll call or show up at inopportune times, ask ridiculous questions, and hound you to death.

The Million-Dollar Question: What Do All Successful Networkers Have in Common?

The envelope, please! Networkers sincerely like people. It's that simple. I bet you expected a complicated answer. It doesn't matter where you hail from—Nebraska, Idaho, Kenya, Vermont—all networkers sincerely like people. If you're genetically hostile or belligerent, or simply have an aversion to most homo sapiens, you had better change your ways. And, when you land a job, your people skills should be razor-sharp. You may hate the term *team player,* but the truth is companies want folks who can work together. It's not to create corporate utopia, but rather because teamwork boosts productivity. Countless surveys rank "interpersonal skills" alongside "ability" as vital assets for career success. People skills are especially important when networking yourself into a job.

Now, let's look at the process.

Networking Is an Informal Process

Don't let anyone tell you there are procedures and rules for good networking. The real pros go at it instinctively. Networking is an informal process with an implied vision. What makes the process so exciting is that each person goes about networking differently, according to his or her individual style.

One thing is certain: Networking is serious business. Make no mistake about it, the winners go at it with a vengeance. Great networking is anything but a hit-or-miss proposition. If done right, it significantly reduces the length of a job search. Supersalesman Harvey Mackay summed up the essence of fruitful networking in his book *Sharkproof:* "It's not who you know and it's not what you know, but what who you know knows."

In *How to Find Your Life's Work,* Richard J. Pilder and William F. Pilder contend that networking is a fluid process or continuum that's always evolving and assuming new shapes and forms. "A network is a structure of relationships through which information and ideas flow in constant motion," they say.

But when you translate all the rhetoric, the essence of networking is an unflagging belief that people are the ultimate key to career success. No matter how smart you are, you *can't* do it alone.

ADVICE

Keep your networking antennae up at all times. Whether you've got the ultimate job or you're on the brink of personal bankruptcy, never stop networking.

STRATEGY: Networking must become part of your lifestyle.

The Secret of Great Networking

Another heavy truth: The foundation of productive networking is *reciprocity.* That means unselfishly sharing information. Skilled networkers never question the fact that they'll be paid back in some way for a good turn. It's understood. It's not you do this for me and, in return, I expect a payback. In short, good networking is based on a timeless adage, "One good turn deserves another."

Network-Building Techniques

Now that you've got a better understanding of what networking is all about, here are a few valuable network-building tips.

Find the King-Makers

What's a king-maker? Maybe you've never heard the term, but I guarantee you know plenty of them. They're everywhere. Virtually every organization has at least one. These powerful people sit at the information hub. News starts with them and filters out to everyone else. Olympic-caliber networker Victor Lindquist, former director of Northwestern University's Placement Center, coined the term. Unlike most of us, king-makers are strategically positioned to attract information and know about events before they happen. They've taken networking to the next level. It's because they're trusted by everyone. It's no wonder they hold power-wielding positions in companies and government. Rest assured, the president's top advisers are king-makers sine qua non. Information starts and stops with them. If someone told them the meaning of life in confidence, torture couldn't pry it from their lips.

If a king-maker likes and trusts you, he or she will help you. If you're lucky, one day you'll get a call late at night that may sound like this, "John, this is Karen Infogod. I apologize for calling so late, but I've got some important news I think you'd like to hear. Dynamic Torpedoes has just created a new systems division and is looking for software engineers. Tommy Twaddlebrain, a senior engineer at Torpedoes, is doing the hiring. He happens to be a good friend of mine so I told him about you. If I were you, I'd give him a call at 8 a.m. tomorrow. By the way John, this news just broke. The headhunters don't even know about it."

Sound farfetched? It's not. This is the kind of exclusive information king-makers provide. There are real-life examples of the above conversation taking place every day. Needless to say, the king-makers in your life deserve to be treated like family, maybe better.

Join Professional Associations

If you've never been a joiner, it would be wise to change this instant. If you hope to build a career, it's essential to plug into every possible information source that can keep you current with your industry. Simply, it means joining professional or trade associations. Since professional organizations are hotbeds of industry and entrepreneurial scuttlebutt, I'm amazed job searchers don't pursue them more often. Cynthia Chin-Lee, author of *It's Who You Know: Career Strategies for Making Effective Personal Contacts,* has been milking information from professional associations for better than a decade. In fact, she landed her first job out of graduate school from a lead she picked up at an Asian Business League meeting in San Francisco.

You say you have no time to be active in professional associations. That's a lame excuse. Make the time. You ought to be on your professional association's mailing list so you will receive bulletins and newsletters. Hook up with members who can fill you in on news from meetings you can't attend. But make sure you set up a reciprocal arrangement with a colleague. You attend a meeting one month, he or she attends a session the next. This way information can be swapped. Everyone wins and you have added a new person to your network.

For example, working women are foolish not to check out *The Business Women's Network Directory,* profiling the top 400 business and professional women's organizations in the United States. With more than 57 million working women nationwide, the number of professional women's organizations has increased dramatically over the last decade. With those powerful numbers, the directory is a must for every woman building a career.

If you ever doubted the power of women's professional associations, look at the formidable numbers of the top 24 women's organizations provided by *Working Woman* magazine:

Top 24 Organizations by Membership

	Organization	*Members*
1.	National Association for Female Executives	250,000
2.	American Nurses Association	200,000
3.	American Association of University Women	135,000
4.	American Business Women's Association	90,000
5.	Soroptimist	95,000
6.	Zonta International	36,000
7.	National Federation of Business and Professional Women	80,000
8.	American Agri Women	35,000
9.	Coalition of Labor Union Women	20,000
10.	Altrusa	18,000
11.	National Association of Insurance Women	15,000
12.	9 to 5 National Association of Working Women	15,000
13.	Society of Women Engineers	15,000
14.	Women's Council of Realtors	14,000
15.	American Medical Women's Association	12,000
16.	Financial Women International	11,000
17.	Women in Communications	10,000
18.	National Association of Negro Business & Professional Women's Clubs	10,000
19.	American Society of Women Accountants	7,000
20.	National Association of Women in Construction	7,000
21.	National Coalition of 100 Black Women	7,000
22.	National Association of Women Business Owners	6,000
23.	Ms. Foundation	6,000
24.	Association of Women in Science	5,000
		Total = 1,099,000

Investigate Formal Networking Groups

Caution: There are networking groups and there are networking groups. Many are a waste of time. But there are many sophisticated groups that can be a wonderful information source. Networking groups are popping up in churches, synagogues, and YMCAs. Most are informal groups in which job searchers exchange information. A few, more formal groups are run by career counselors or outplacement professionals.

Over the past decade colleges and universities have been expanding their alumni networking services. These are definitely worth exploring. To whet your appetite, here is a sampling of programs.

- Bryant College in Smithfield, RI, has an alumni network program called "First Year on the Job: What It's Really Like" in which employed graduates give talks on job finding.
- Syracuse University in Syracuse, NY, offers timely job tips and 60 internships.
- Cornell University in Ithaca, NY, provides networking opportunities during frequently scheduled "Career Nights" in Boston, New York, Philadelphia, Chicago, San Francisco, and Los Angeles.
- The University of Pennsylvania's Trustees Council of Penn Women in Philadelphia recently kicked off a phone mentoring program. Recent female grads can call alums to get inside information about a specific field.
- The American Graduate School of International Management, popularly known as Thunderbird, in Phoenix, AZ, offers a unique networking opportunity for alums called "First Tuesday." On the first Tuesday of every month, 22,000 alums of Thunderbird, the largest graduate business school in the United States, meet to network at designated spots (usually favorite watering holes or restaurants) in major cities throughout the country. Call Thunderbird graduates and they'll tell you where the meetings will be held. Alums tout the events as

worthwhile for picking up job tips. One alum, who found his current job through a First Tuesday lead, said "Thunderbird grads like to hire other Thunderbird grads. It's been that way since the 1940s."

- The mentoring program of the University of Southern California's School of Business Administration in Los Angeles connects 9000 MBA alumni throughout the world.
- The ASK (Alumni Sharing Knowledge) program of Washington University's Olin School of Business in St. Louis, MO, gives alums a raft of job particulars (qualifications, preparation, occupational outlook, advancement, training, salaries, and benefits).
- The University of Florida (Gainesville) has a successful networking system boasting job placements at prestigious firms such as brokerage house Goldman Sachs, consulting firm Arthur Andersen, and Fortune 500 companies Philip Morris and General Mills.

In addition, profit-making companies, such as Exec-U-Net in Weston, CT, sell networking services. The company has five locations and 2000 members who pay annual dues of $260 to receive what Exec-U-Net president David Opton swears is an exclusive 20-page newsletter offering 150 job leads. Opton says the leads come from exclusive sources such as headhunting firms, and none of the jobs have been advertised. He also insists that seven out of ten executives who change jobs do so through networking opportunities. It sounds enticing, but remember who's spouting these compelling statistics.

ADVICE

Before reaching for your checkbook to pay for networking services, do some investigating. Speak to clients and find out if it resulted in a job, or at least fabulous leads.

Seven Networking Commandments

To sum up, following are seven commandments for successful networking.

1. *Network daily and set goals.* Never lose touch with people. Don't wait until you're in trouble.

   Set networking goals. Make 10 networking calls a day. Consider these numbers. If you make 10 calls a day, that's 50 calls a week or 200 calls a month. The law of averages says that by doing so you'll add at least a dozen valuable links to your networking chain. Keep that up throughout your career and you'll have one hell of an impressive network.
2. *Information is everywhere.* Keep an open mind and realize that information might turn up in unlikely places. You might stumble on a priceless networking contact in a hotel lobby, bar, airport, or bus station or even at a family gathering. Even vacations may produce some surprising networking opportunities.
3. *Everyone is reachable.* Start out with a healthy attitude toward people in power. Don't think someone is off-limits because she has an impressive job. Everyone is reachable if you keep at it. The challenging part is breaking through the fortresslike structures by befriending the gatekeepers. They're the ones who'll pry open the doors to the inner circle. It may take a while, but don't give up. It's worth investing weeks trying to reach an influential lead.
4. *Be persistent.* As R. David Thomas, president and founder of Wendy's International, said in his biography, *Dave's Way:* "Don't expect anything to come easy. If you want something, go after it and don't give up." In short, persistence pays off. Don't be unreasonable and expect every networking contact to be a platinum lead. Some will be worthwhile while others won't. You won't know which until you run them all down. Don't be lazy and give up when leads aren't panning out. The worst kind of networking is the fitful variety.
5. *Be direct and sincere.* Be direct, truthful, and straightforward with people with whom you hope to network. The surest way to

sabotage your networking machinery is to resort to underhanded tactics. People are more tuned in than you may realize.

6. *Never forget a good turn.* Be gracious. When someone does you a good turn, acknowledge it immediately. Rather than just calling, Cynthia Chin-Lee advises sending a letter first. In her view, if people take time out of a busy schedule to help her, they deserve the courtesy of a written acknowledgment. When a networking lead results in a job, she takes the person out to lunch or dinner.
7. *Keep a networking diary.* Last, but by no means least, keep a networking diary or journal. I urge you to do it in your computer, where you can easily add or delete names and keep detailed notes to update regularly. Record keeping is a drag. Nevertheless, it's worth your while to discipline yourself and keep this information up to date. Ideally, your journal is not just a diary, but a database as well. You should have the name, address, and phone numbers of every contact. Every meeting should be meticulously noted so your impressions and insights are chronicled. Unless you have a photographic memory, you cannot keep all this information in your head.

   Don't make too much of keeping a diary. Entries can be brief and written in shorthand, full of typos and misspellings. They are going to be read only by you.

   Consider this sample notation.

Week ending December 15, 1996

December 11: Met Harry Spiegel, JoAnn Tarantino's lead. Helpful guy who gave me dirt on Justified Grenades. Learned company is in deep s—t and considering Chapter 11. He told me to call him after the first of the year and he'll hook me up with Clyde McFadder, senior VP at Pungent Gas. Could be a good lead. McFadder is an aggressive guy who'll do anything to further his career. Big point.

December 14: Fast afterwork drink with David Afghan-Bozo, who wants me to call him at end of January to find out about potential jobs at Driscol Destroyers, supposedly a hot, well-financed armaments firm. He's waiting on his lead to give him further details on contacts and conditions of company. Could be hot opportunity.

You get the idea. Keep your diary current and you won't be left in the dark.

ADVICE

Record impressions within 5 hours of meeting someone. This way, you won't forget important details. Let too much time pass and you're bound to leave out important details.

One last word: Don't get discouraged. Compiling a tight network is a long, tedious process. Think of it in terms of building a stock portfolio that will pay off handsomely in the future. *Remember:* Most employers would rather fill jobs through networking than endure the expense of running newspaper ads, sifting through résumés, or dealing with employment agencies. *Best news of all:* When you walk into an interview because someone recommended you, you have an immediate leg up on the situation. If that doesn't make networking worthwhile, I don't know what does.

Let's pick up the beat and check out the job market.

CHAPTER 11

CHECKING OUT THE JOB ACTION

RULE 11 **Don't believe everything you read. There are jobs in virtually every sector of the market.**

Don't let anyone tell you there are no available jobs. You'll be pleasantly surprised to find that more job opportunities exist than you realize. And there are definitely some surprises and hidden jewels you didn't know about.

Let's take it from the top and get the conservative reading from our national forecasters, the smart economists at the U.S. Department of Labor's Bureau of Labor Statistics (BLS).

According to the BLS, total employment through 1995 is projected to increase by 14 percent (17.7 million), from 127.0 million in 1994 to 144.7 million in 2005.

Break down these statistics and here's where you'll find most of the jobs.

- Service-producing industries will account for virtually all job growth. Only construction will add jobs in the goods-producing sector.
- Manufacturing's share of total jobs is expected to decline by a decrease of 1.3 million jobs. Manufacturing is expected to maintain its share of total output, as productivity in this sector is projected to increase. Accounting for one of every seven jobs in 1994, manufacturing is expected to account for just less than one in eight jobs by 2005.

- Health, business, and social services are expected to account for almost one of every two jobs added to the economy through 2005.
- Professional specialty occupations are projected to increase the fastest and add the most jobs—more than 5 million. This group also had the fastest increase rate and the largest job growth in the 1983–1994 period. Service workers are expected to add 4.6 million jobs. These two groups—on opposite ends of the educational and earnings spectrum—are expected to provide more than half of the total projected job growth for the next decade.
- Other groups projected to grow faster than the average are executive, administrative, and managerial occupations; technicians and related support occupations; and marketing and sales occupations.

Top 10 Industries with Fastest Job Growth (Through 2005)

1. Health services
2. Residential care
3. Computer and data processing services
4. Individual and miscellaneous social services
5. Miscellaneous business services
6. Child-care services
7. Personnel supply services
8. Services to buildings
9. Miscellaneous equipment rental and leasing
10. Management and public relations

Top 10 Fastest-Growing Occupations (Through 2005)

1. Personal and home-care aides
2. Home-health aides
3. Systems analysts
4. Computer engineers
5. Physical and corrective therapy assistants and aides
6. Electronic pagination systems workers

7. Occupational therapy assistants and aides
8. Physical therapists
9. Residential counselors
10. Human service workers

Top 10 Occupations with the Largest Job Growth (Through 2005)

1. Cashiers
2. Janitors and cleaners, including maids and housekeeping cleaners
3. Salespersons, retail
4. Waiters and waitresses
5. Registered nurses
6. General managers and top executives
7. Systems analysts
8. Home-health aides
9. Guards
10. Nurse's aides, orderlies, and attendants

The above statistics capture the national trends. But there's a lot more going on. Here are 19 hot job tracks mentioned in *U.S. News & World Report* that are worth exploring

1. *Accounting.* What with U.S. companies opening divisions all over the world, international accountants are needed to negotiate deals and supervise the numbers. Companies need accountants who know international financial reporting, merger and acquisition protocol, and foreign business customs. The number of accountants at major firms has increased four- and fivefold in the past 5 years. The trend is expected to continue for the next 5 years as well.
2. *Architecture.* In the old days, architects designed buildings and contractors built them. The new trend is hiring one company to handle the whole process. These workers are called design/build specialists. It's a consolidation of services, saving the client a pile of dough. Architectural firms offer a package

deal, supplying both design and building services under one roof. The Design/Build Institute of America reports that 28 percent of new nonresidential buildings are now put up through the design/build process, a jump of 10 percent. By 2005, it could account for nearly 50 percent. A related track with an exciting future includes the high-tech home or office specialists. Also called ergonomic specialists, they design the workspaces that allow human and technical gadgets to work compatibly.

3. *Consulting.* If you're wondering who's reeingineering American corporations, it's the growing army of consultants, many of whom are corporate refugees. As companies continue to grow leaner and meaner, consultants' ranks increase exponentially.
4. *Education.* As America becomes a true melting pot society, the demand for bilingual teachers increases. About 100 languages are spoken in the U.S. school system. If you're fluent in Spanish and English, you can literally work in any school system in the country.

   If you've got the stomach for the corporate world, companies with international divisions also need bilingual workers. As companies become more global, the demand is expected to increase.

   There's also a big demand for special-education teachers. The National Clearinghouse for Professions in Special Education reports that schools need 30,000 more special-ed teachers to work with emotionally disturbed and learning-disabled kids.
5. *Engineering.* Regardless of economic trends, engineers have always managed to eke out a decent living. The hot engineering field these days centers on software design. Since 1982, average software sales have been up 27 percent yearly. Robust sales are projected through the year 2000 and beyond. A decade ago, a computer was a luxury; today it's a necessity in both home and office. No wonder programming must be constantly upgraded to perform bigger and more impressive tasks. The demand for

software engineers far exceeds the supply of recent graduates. Carnegie Mellon University, for example, reported recruitment of software engineers jumped 20 percent last year.

With an aggressive push to clean up the environment, environmental engineers are also finding plenty of work.

6. *Entertainment.* Every industry is making good use of the computer. The entertainment moguls are no different. Whether it's a sci-fi, horror, or fantasy flick the likes of *Jurassic Park,* the film industry has jumped on computer animation and computer graphics in a big way. As the price of computer animation software drops, it's expected to play an even bigger role in the future. Commercial filmmakers are not the only ones jumping on computer graphics. Industrial filmmakers are taking advantage of it too, creating many more jobs.
7. *Environment.* It wasn't too long ago cartographers could make decent money drawing maps. Not any longer. You're behind the times if you use a pencil and slide rule. Now everything's done on the computer with Geographic Information Systems (GIS) software. The whole thing can be done in living color more precisely and faster. It's not just map designers that are using this software, but city planning commissions contemplating building bridges, tunnels, and roads as well as manufacturers laying the groundwork for new factories and mills. In 1994, sales of GIS software hit $760 million worldwide. Through 1999, they're expected to grow by 12 percent a year.
8. *Finance.* Thanks to inflation and an exorbitantly high cost of living, socking money away in a savings account is not going to get you very far. Like it or not, wage earners, especially those with college-bound children, have no choice but to creatively invest their money. Hence, they're looking to brokerage and investment banking houses and small financial-planning firms for advice. Solid demand for these professionals is projected through 2000.
9. *Health-care administration.* It's no secret that health-care costs will continue to go through the roof until a remedy is

found. Meanwhile, hospitals and health-care organizations are trimming costs and eliminating paperwork by electronically storing records and files. The computer wizards who manage all this electronic data are called information specialists. Besides cutting staff and bookkeeping costs, electronic records can be retrieved faster, allowing physicians access to records thousands of miles away. The demand for experienced professionals is expected to outpace supply by 54 percent by 2000.

10. *Hospitality.* A growing number of Americans are working longer and harder than in the past and no longer have time to prepare supper at home. They're either eating out or ordering in. That explains why the food service industry takes about 44 cents of every dollar spent on food. The good news is jobs in food service management will leap 44 percent by 2005, according to the Bureau of Labor Statistics. That means restaurants, hotels, and contract food service companies will be hiring food service managers to purchase food and supplies, plan menus, and supervise operations.

    Thanks to a favorable outlook for the travel industry over the next few years, there will also be a demand for hotel managers to oversee hotel operations.

11. *Human services.* As the government continues to close mental institutions, group homes have sprung up to deliver residential and counseling services to former prisoners and troubled teens. Residential counselors supervise and analyze clients' needs and offer emotional and support counseling.

    A relatively new job slot with a promising outlook is that of a life skills instructor to help developmentally disabled clients master everyday skills from cooking to using public transportation.

12. *Information services.* The extraordinary growth projected for the Internet means a slew of exciting new career options. One new title is webmaster, a cyberpro who designs and maintains a company's World Wide Web site. The demand for this skill will accelerate as more companies develop home pages. The webmaster's job functions include managing the editorial and

graphic content of the page as well as the associated public relations and marketing message.

13. *Law.* Over the past few years, the Equal Opportunity Commission has been deluged with thousands of sexual harassment claims. Since more workers are willing to file complaints, lawyers on both sides of the fence have more work than they can handle. The high-paying jobs can be found in the large law firms. The smaller firms offer excellent salaries as well.

    There is also a dramatic increase in the demand for paralegals specializing in EEOC complaints.

14. *Media.* Some futurists insist that conventional print publications will go the way of the dinosaur. That's farfetched, but one thing is certain: Electronic newspapers, magazines, and newsletters are growing rapidly. Five years ago, they didn't exist. Now there are about 500, and media experts predict that number will quadruple over the next few years. On-line content developers write stories, commission journalists to write for the publication, and repackage previously published material.

15. *Wireless services.* Try to explain this job area to a technophobic person. The demand for wireless technology, mobile cordless phones, and fax machines, pagers, and beepers increases only as new models hit the market and prices drop. If you've got selling talent, here's a blue-chip career for the millennium.

16. *Science research.* Bet you didn't know almost half of the human body's 80,000 genes have been located. Each new discovery means pharmaceuticals companies can search for treatments for killer diseases like cancer, diabetes, and AIDS. Drug companies, government labs, and research think tanks need genetic researchers with the potential to stop diseases in their tracks.

17. *Social work.* The numbers speak for themselves. By the year 2025, the number of people 85 and over (at about 3.5 million now) will more than double. Geriatric case managers will be needed to evaluate the health of elderly clients and provide advice on everything from living arrangements to financial and legal aid.

18. *Sports management.* Here's a fun career for people who love sports and have selling ability. Sports sponsorship, the financing of events and teams, is a powerful niche industry all its own. Last year, North American companies spent a whopping $3.05 billion on sports sponsorships, a jump of 44 percent since 1992. Sharp-tongued salespeople are needed to cut these megadeals.
19. *Telecommunications.* Wherever money is being made, you're bound to find less than honest folks hot to get their hands on it. With the explosion of traffic on the Internet and the runaway growth of computer networks, cyberthieves have been doing their best to get an illegal piece of the action. At the moment, they've bitten off about a $9 billion chunk, a number which is expected to increase dramatically over the next few years. Companies are hiring experienced cybersleuths to install software that can be protected with constant password changes and to design encryption techniques that convert classified information into indecipherable code.

More Super Hot Jobs

- *Computer engineer.* The job carries a whopping projected growth rate (through 2005) of 112 percent. Computer engineers develop and design hardware and software. Their skills are needed in virtually every corner of the economy, from business software and microchips that trigger a car's air bags to video and computer games.
- *Systems analysts.* This job title boasts an equally impressive growth rate of 110 percent. Systems analysts define business, scientific, or engineering problems and design solutions using computers.
- *Virtual reality programmer.* Once a trendy gadget of the entertainment industry, virtual reality technology is now being used by architects, industrial engineers, and automotive designers. Virtual reality software allows you to take a trip

through a factory or corporate headquarters or to test a car before it's even built.

- *Allied health professionals.* As we said earlier, the projections for health-care professionals couldn't be better. The U.S. Bureau of Labor Statistics (BLS) reports that one out of every two new jobs created by the year 2005 will be in the health-care field. Additionally, changes in the health-care system combined with an aging population will trigger aggressive growth in the health-related occupations, according to the BLS. By the year 2025, older Americans will outnumber teenagers by a two-to-one ratio.

It's no wonder one-third of the 30 fastest-growing occupations are projected to be health-related, and health-care related curriculums are attracting people from many different backgrounds. Stockbrokers, construction workers, and corporate executives, for example, are switching to health-care fields because the demand is high and the future looks good. Equally important, the field is changing rapidly. New fields are popping up all the time. Colleges are responding to the demand for health-care professionals by offering a smorgasbord of programs. A decade ago, the demand for nurses, especially registered nurses (RNs), far surpassed the supply. What with cutbacks in government funding and the proliferation of managed-care organizations (HMOs), hospitals and other health-care providers have cut their nursing budgets. Recent nursing grads are having a tougher time finding jobs in hospitals, yet hospitals are still hiring experienced RNs. Nevertheless, the demand for nurses is still excellent. Hospitals may have cut back hiring, but nursing homes, HMOs, and home-care agencies have picked up the slack.

There is a particularly strong demand for nurses with advanced degrees. RNs with additional education and certification can write their own career ticket. The hot nursing specialty is nurse practitioner (NP). NPs can provide about 85 percent of the care required for patients coming into a general practitioner's office. They can assess a patient, do diagnoses, prescribe treatment, and write prescriptions.

And they can work in many health-care settings, especially growing specialties like adult and family practice, pediatrics, gerontology, AIDS, and women's health. With advanced training, the nurse practitioner is well positioned to work in tomorrow's demanding workplace.

There are many other health fields with similarly exciting job outlooks. The demand for physician assistants (PAs), for example, has increased dramatically. Working under the direction of physicians, PAs are responsible for the day-to-day care of patients. In some states they have more latitude than nurses.

There is also a strong demand for physical therapists. The American Hospital Association reports a 15 percent vacancy rate in this field.

Two other hot allied health-care specialties are nutritionists and dental hygienists. With more people concerned with eating properly, losing weight, and staying healthy, nutritionists are needed in hospitals, health spas, and gyms. The demand for dental hygienists is equally exciting. The BLS projects a 41 percent increase, or 40,000 new jobs, through the year 2005. Dental hygienists are needed in dental practices and dental manufacturing companies, as well as in hospitals, nursing homes, and public health agencies.

Look around and you'll find plenty of other jobs that are just as exciting.

ADVICE

Veer off the conventional job highway and explore seldom-tread roads. You never know what gold mine opportunities lurk in the shadows. The next few chapters explore a few of them.

CHAPTER 12

THE TRUTH ABOUT HUMAN RESOURCES FOLKS, PLACEMENT MANAGERS, AND HEADHUNTERS

RULE 12 Keep your options open by pursuing all job-hunting leads.

We've been programmed to expect far too much of human resource professionals, employment agencies, and headhunters. Let's take a fresh look at each so you know realistically what to expect.

Let's start with the good folks who run human resources departments. If you've never worked for a large company, you've missed out on complicated bureaucratic hiring in all its glory. The people who do the picking of applicants are called human resources (HR) professionals or managers. Until the profession gained respectability 20 years ago, these staffers were just known as personnel workers. Today, I'm sorry to say, they wield a lot of power. Unless it's an executive being recruited for a high-level job slot, a process which requires care and attention by several departments, the hiring process begins with an HR person (who perfunctorily checks to see if you're breathing, walking, and capable of making a decent impression). This person's job could be on the line if he or she recommends a hyperkinetic drooler or serial killer. The HR person's job ends as soon as you are passed on to the next person in the hiring process. If you're being considered for a job in a large company, you could have as many as three or four interviews before you're hired.

Don't underestimate the power of HR departments. Remember, they receive thousands of résumés from eager job hunters like yourself. The average midsize company receives 200,000 to 300,000 résumés a year. And they're all sent to some faceless worker in the HR department. At the bottom of a typical want ad in a newspaper, you'll find a name and address reading something like this: "Send all résumés to Ms. Brunhilda Smolett-Himler, Human Resources Manager, Heindruk Botcher Ltd."

Sorry to disappoint you, but the Smolett-Himlers out there seldom clap eyes on résumés. In fact, they couldn't care less if you're a budding Bill Gates capable of turning the company into a zillion-dollar enterprise overnight. The pile of résumés growing in the HR department is perused by one of Smolett-Himler's assistants, who screens résumés all day long. More on the résumé-screening process later. Suffice it to say, HR people don't spend a lot of time reading each résumé. Forget about all the hard work it took to get that résumé looking like a veritable Picasso on 8"×10" paper. *The HR folks don't care.* Their job is to scan every résumé for *certain* qualifications. If the right words don't jump out at them in the space of 30 seconds, the résumé is tossed in the reject pile, where its owner is slated to receive an "official" reject letter on company stationery. It will read like this:

> Dear Mr. Sorrysack Cleptowack: Thank you for considering us. Unfortunately, your qualifications, while impressive, don't match the specifications for the position of manager of our high-tech toothpick division. Nevertheless, we're keeping your résumé on file, should a suitable position open up.

The note sounds so polite, you almost feel like thanking them for being considerate enough to respond with such a thoughtful rejection letter. You may not have secured an interview, but you got the next best thing. They're going to keep your résumé on file. Fantastic.

If you're dumb enough to believe a letter like that, I'll never let you read another one of my books. The truth is they're not keeping your résumé on file. From the reject pile, your résumé goes directly to the company's résumé purgatory, where it sits until a few thousand more résumés are piled on top. When it becomes a towering weighty pile, the next and last stop is the company trash bins. Sorry if I ruined your day Mr. Cleptowack. You struck out.

ADVICE

Take the hint. Don't waste time corresponding with HR departments.

Strategy for Getting Jobs in Midsize and Large Companies

Just because I've trashed HR departments doesn't mean you should turn your back on job opportunities in midsize and large companies. The moral of the above diatribe is you should find a better way to get your foot in the door. I'm sorry to say there are no pat solutions.

STRATEGY: The only way to reach the right people is by employing ingenuity and doing some detective work. Bypass the HR cyborgs by finding out who is actually doing the hiring. HR departments do what they're told. They get a formal job request from a manager and immediately search for someone with the right credentials. But no one says you can't cut off the HR folks at the pass by finding out what a manager is looking for and then corresponding with him or her directly. It's done every day. In fact, managers prefer this method because it makes their lives easier, especially if you're perfect for the job. You score immediately by making a great impression. "Hey, I like her style. She wants a job and goes right after it. I wish I had used that tactic when I was pounding the pavement."

I Suppose You're Going to Tell Me Hiring Information Grows on Trees, Right?

I never said it did. Nevertheless, getting inside hiring information is not as difficult as you might think. The best way is contacting someone you know who works at the company or at least a friend of a friend or a relative. Did you forget about your professional association or network? Peruse the lengthy list of names comprising your network and I guarantee bells will go off in your head. "Why didn't I think of Ginny Attlebrain-Schlag? She's been running their cranberry-crushing unit for almost 10 years."

Where there is a will, there is a way. Now the straight poop on employment agencies.

Employment Agencies: A Blessing or a Curse? "Don't Call Me a Flesh Peddler, Okay!"

Employment agencies can be a blessing or a curse. They can be a valuable part of a job search. But if you rely on them to find you a job, you're playing a dangerous game.

Employment agencies earn money by getting people jobs. Agency interviewers are called placement managers. By the mid-1970s, disenchanted and angry applicants tagged such managers as "flesh peddlers," because they aggressively hustled bodies into jobs with little concern about whether it was an appropriate fit. A competitive job market, tougher employer demands, and fewer orders have since prompted agencies to improve that image.

STRATEGY: Locate an agency that can help you. Find the ones that cater to your field. Start by perusing the want ads and then consider purchasing *The National Directory of Personnel Consultants,* published by the National Association of Personnel Consultants (3133

Mount Vernon Avenue, Alexandria, VA 22305). Save time by taking advantage of its geographic and specialty listings.

Don't Get Your Hopes Up

It's often the luck of the draw when it comes to working with agencies. It's especially true if you're in a popular field in which one want ad may draw 300 to 500 résumés. The odds can be unbelievable. Even more frightening, five agencies may have the same job listing, making the odds even higher.

WARNING: Employment agencies are seldom useful for obscure fields. If you have a master's or doctorate degree in art history, geophysics, ornithology, nuclear physics, or horticulture, for example, chances are employment agencies won't be able to help you. It's a question of supply and demand. Agencies traditionally serve fields in which the demand for skills and the supply of workers are high.

ADVICE

Tread carefully. Employment agencies ought to be only one component of your job-hunting strategy. This way, you're not totally dependent on them for finding you a job.

Check out the office. A busy employment agency can resemble a railroad station. A crowded, active office is a good omen. It means the agency has lots of jobs and contacts. The more interviews it can send you on, the better your odds of finding something quickly.

Don't be put off if a placement manager seems gruff and harried. You'd be the same way if you held this pressure-cooker job. This overworked person is competing with many other agencies servicing the same field. If he doesn't place a pile of people, he doesn't eat. After all, the job pool is just so large.

CHAPTER TWELVE

Three All-Purpose Tips for Dealing with Employment Agencies

1. *Visit the agency.* Personal contact is vital. Avoid having a purely phone relationship with an agency. Otherwise, you're just a voice. The average placement manager may speak to 50 people in a business day. It can be difficult distinguishing you from the many other applicants searching for the same kind of job. Make a point to schedule an appointment and meet with this person. It's worth the effort because it will then be easier for the manager to tie the voice to the face.

   Some agencies require face-to-face meetings with applicants before sending them on interviews. That's a good sign. It means the agency has a close relationship with its clients and is being cautious. The firm's not going to send just anyone out on interviews. It is protecting itself and saving time by doing the initial screening.

2. *Interview the manager.* Don't just let the agency people interview you; interview *them* as well. Get a sense of whether this agency can help you. A brief conversation can reveal a lot. If the interaction doesn't feel right, find another agency. There are plenty from which to choose.

   Ask questions. What kind of companies does the agency work with? Who does the manager work with—human resource departments, managers, or division heads? How long has the agency been working with the company? Has it placed other people there? Does the agency have an exclusive contract with the company?

3. *Carefully scrutinize any contracts or agreements you're asked to sign.* In metropolitan areas, 98 percent of the placement fees are paid by employers. The fee can range from 10 to 20 percent of your first year's salary. In some jurisdictions, it's governed by state law. Sometimes, you'll be required to pay all or part of the fee. Here are some of the fee arrangements you may face:

- Applicant-paid fees: You pay the entire fee.
- Partial-paid fees: Prior to job acceptance, you and the employer negotiate and each pays part of the fee.
- Fee reimbursed by employer: You initially pay the fee, but the employer agrees to reimburse you after a certain period of time on the job.
- Fee reimbursed by employee: The employer pays the fee initially and deducts the amount from the employee's paycheck over a period of time.
- Partial fee reimbursed by employer: The employer agrees to reimburse a portion of the fee after a stipulated time period.

Keep in Touch

Once you've signed with an agency, maintain close contact. Don't be a pest and call every day. A call every 2 weeks, however, is perfectly okay.

Busy managers have more clients than they can handle. It's easy to get lost in the files if no immediate jobs are right for you. By constantly reminding the manager of your availability, you stand a better chance of being sent on interviews.

ADVICE

Get as much exposure as possible by registering with many agencies serving your field. One agency's contacts may be better than another's. But also bear in mind that it's easy to lose track of where your résumés are sent when you register with several agencies. *Solution:* Keep a log of where and when you send your résumés, as well as your agency contacts. This way you'll always be on top of the situation.

When an agency gets you an interview, find out everything you can about the company so you don't walk in cold. Know what the company does, what job is open, what the job responsibilities are, and what kind of future it holds.

Don't expect the placement manager to supply all the answers either. Do some legwork on your own. If it's a publicly held company, plenty of information is available. You can look at current annual reports or check *Moody's* or *Standard & Poor's*. See if there are any recent news articles about the firm. The more you know, the better the impression you'll make. Most important, you'll be ready to make an intelligent decision if you are offered a job.

Now the skinny on headhunters.

Meet the Headhunters [Executive Search Firms]

It's a definite source of confusion. Many job hunters mistakenly think employment agencies are headhunters or executive search firms. Let's clear the air once and for all. In contrast to employment agencies, search firms, often called retainer firms, deal exclusively with companies rather than applicants. Their client is the *company,* not the applicant.

Search firms concentrate on finding executives at the supervisory, middle-management, and senior-management levels. Salaries range from $65,000 to $500,000 and more for chief executive officer slots. The search firm's job is to research, find, and recruit the best person for a management-level job. The firm is paid a retainer, which is about 33 percent of the executive's first-year salary, regardless of whether it finds the right person. Search firms are called "headhunters" because of the aggressive networking methods used to find applicants. When tracking down suitable candidates, headhunters can be likened to private detectives. Their salaries are on a par with, and often exceed, those of the executives they place. As a rule, don't expect to strike up a lifelong friendship with most headhunters.

Because of the power they wield, most are abrupt, officious, aloof, hard-to-reach, and virtual prima donnas.

Jim Kennedy, editor and publisher of the New Hampshire-based *Executive Recruiter News* and the *Directory of Executive Recruiters,* says job hunters expect too much of search firms. If you happen to match some or all of the specifications of an assignment they're trying to fill, you've hit the jackpot. If not, *don't give up.* It doesn't cost that much to correspond with as many executive search firms as you think might be able to help you.

The *1996 Guide to Executive Recruiters* by Michael Betrus (McGraw-Hill) and Kennedy's *Directory of Executive Recruiters* (updated yearly) list recruiters alphabetically, by industry and location. In a few moments, you can find every search firm serving your industry.

Here are a few suggestions that will help you work with search firms.

1. *Don't visit search firms.* You're wasting your time. It's inappropriate and the chances are slim you'll get to talk to a search executive.
2. *Don't expect any acknowledgment if you write or call.* They're not being rude, they just don't have the time or resources to respond to every résumé and letter they receive. If you send your résumé (or a letter alternative, which I'll discuss later) to a search firm and it's applicable to some of the fields in which the firm does business, there's an excellent chance the firm will get back to you. But if you just randomly mail to a handful of search firms, you're wasting time and money. You'd do better targeting your correspondence to firms that may be able to help you.
3. *Maintain contact with search firms.* As long as you're in the job market, keep corresponding with search firms every 3 to 6 months. Many search firms discard résumés and letters after a couple of months. Don't assume you're permanently on file. You never know when a call for your particular qualifications will come in.

4. *Make sure you pay no fee.* If the search firm tries to charge you a fee, it is not an ethical firm. Many counseling firms erroneously call themselves search firms and charge applicants fees for their services. From the onset, know what type of organization you're dealing with.

Let's uncover some hidden leads you've never considered.

CHAPTER 13

HIDDEN MARKET FINDS NO ONE TALKS ABOUT

INCUBATORS, ENTERPRISE ZONES, SBDCs, AND OTHER GEMS

Look beneath the surface and you'll find seldom-explored job-hunting leads.

Just look around and you'll find "gold in them thar hills." There are plenty of off-the-beaten-track leads that career writers call the hidden job market. I'm not going to go off on a tangent praising the benefits of tapping into this powerful market. That's already been done countless times by career writers the likes of Richard Bolles in *What Color Is Your Parachute?* and Tom Jackson in *The Hidden Job Market.*

Legend has it the hidden job market accounts for 65 to 90 percent of all available jobs—although no one has come up with any hard numbers to prove this assertion. The published or traditional market consists of want ads in which companies and employment agencies advertise their jobs.

Twenty years ago, the published job market actually resulted in interviews. Not any more. If you rely solely on the published market, you'll be chronically unemployed. It can be likened to playing the lottery. You just might get lucky.

Hidden job market proponents advise pouring all your energy into pursuing unconventional leads. A better strategy is to play *both* markets. What do you have to lose? Let's get into this hidden market stuff more deeply.

What the Heck Is the Hidden Market Anyway?

Simply, if a job isn't published or listed, and most people don't know about it, it's hidden. But there is more to it. The popular hidden job market techniques are networking and pursuing job leads through professional and alumni associations.

But there are other hidden market strategies no one talks about.

Hard Openings versus Soft Openings

A popular hidden job market strategy is finding out who's hiring, firing, or retiring. It doesn't take a genius to know that if an entire department is fired, the company is going to search for a few capable people to do the work of many. The big question is *when.* Barring shake-ups or consolidations, companies will normally hire people within the course of a year as business improves. Whatever the circumstances, the astute job hunter knows most companies don't make quick hiring decisions. The first step is deciding whether it needs more bodies. After that, it's what the job responsibilities are and what the job should pay.

The creation of a job describes the transition from soft to hard opening. A hard opening is an immediately available job, contrasted to a soft opening, which is an evolving, yet undefined position. Soft openings are common after mergers and reorganizations. To trim costs, two or three jobs are consolidated into one. The bigger the company, the longer the transition period from soft to hard opening. New job titles have to be approved and the corporate organization chart has to be reworked. Once the paperwork is finished, it could take several months before the decision makers sign off on the position.

STRATEGY: Use your network to uncover soft openings. Then monitor them so you're in the wings and ready to pounce once they become hard openings. At any given moment, count on thousands of soft openings within every industry. You're ahead of the game if you're monitoring a handful at a time.

Now some solid hidden market sources.

Promising Start-Up Companies Can Be Found in Business Incubators

Don't be embarrassed if you've never heard of a business incubator. First, a little Biology 101. An incubator is an apparatus for the maintenance of controlled conditions. It's a warm environment allowing eggs to hatch or premature babies to grow until they're strong enough to thrive on their own.

Likewise, a business incubator provides start-up companies with a controlled and nurturing environment in which to grow and thrive.

Business incubators house a number of new and emerging businesses under one roof. Each incubator is unique, with facilities ranging in size from 10,000 to more than 400,000 square feet. The median size is about 24,500 square feet. The largest incubator has close to 80 tenants, the median number of tenants is 8.

After 3 to 5 years, businesses expand and leave the incubator because they need larger facilities. Until they're ready to go on their own, the incubator acts as a mother hen providing the following services to fledgling businesses:

- Flexible space and leases, often at below-market rates
- Shared business services such as telephone answering, bookkeeping, word processing, and secretarial help

- Business and technical assistance, including in-house expertise on legal, accounting, marketing, business planning, and engineering problems
- Financial assistance for obtaining bank loans and advice for getting venture capital and federal and state funds

Except for retail, incubators serve virtually all industries, especially high-technology and light-manufacturing industries. Most are operated by nonprofit organizations such as universities, colleges, and community colleges (17 percent); for-profit businesses (14 percent); and economic development agencies, local governments, or a consortium of all these organizations (69 percent).

Tapping a Virgin Market More Incubators Are Sprouting Up

There's good news and bad news. First, the good news. Incubators are a relatively new and growing industry. There are more than 500 business incubators housing 6000-plus tenants throughout the United States, up from just 10 to 15 in 1980. New incubators are opening at a rate of 4 to 5 a month. According to the National Incubator Association of America, by the year 2000, more than 1000 incubators will be operating in the United States.

Many of tomorrow's successful entrepreneurs will come from these incubators. Because of their carefully nurtured beginnings, businesses launched in incubators stand a better chance of surviving than do traditional start-ups. The U.S. Small Business Administration reports that approximately 50 to 75 percent of new businesses fail within the first 3 years. Yet only between 10 and 20 percent of businesses launched in incubators fail within the first 5 years of life. Unlike most businesses, incubator companies start with a built-in life-support system, and thus have a better chance of survival. Put it all together and incubators represent exciting ground-floor job opportunities.

Hook up with a potential fast-track start-up company when it's just opening its doors and you face a potentially hot opportunity. Make yourself invaluable and you could have a ready-made career ahead of you. You're also in an excellent position to share in the profits and become an owner either through receiving stock gifts or buying a piece of the business.

But there is a downside as well. Incubator companies are bare-bones, lean-and-mean, no-frills operations. Most are two- and three-person businesses. When they hire someone, they do so hesitantly. They'll hire one person and expect him or her to do the work of three people. Most incubators don't pay competitive salaries. You're lucky if you do much better than minimum wage. The reasons are obvious. Hell-bent on surviving, incubator companies have mastered the art of doing more with less.

But sweat equity pays off. Not only are you in a strategic position to build a career, you're also going to learn what makes a company tick. There are no prima donnas at these fledgling companies. Count on doing everything, from making decisions to fetching coffee and taking out the trash. In short, if the personal chemistry and vibes are right, it spells blue-chip opportunity. If you have entrepreneurial aspirations, working for an incubator is better than enrolling in an MBA program.

ADVICE

Learn all you can about incubators so you can pursue them with a vengeance.

Finding and Connecting with Incubators

You can find local incubators by checking the sources listed below. Then, research their tenants to find companies that appeal to you.

STRATEGY: Rather than write or call companies that interest you, first contact the incubator's manager. Sidestepping this person could amount to a monumental mistake. Incubator managers are the gatekeepers and carry a lot of clout with tenants. Incubator managers also double as business counselors. They're in the best position to give you inside information about which companies offer potential career opportunities. Ask specific questions about the company's products or services, length of time in the incubator, number of employees, background, and so on. Strike up a rapport with an incubator manager and she may identify the saints and lunatics for you.

FAR-OUT STRATEGY FOR RISK TAKERS: If you're among the small army of well-heeled job searchers booted from the corporate arena with generous severance packages, consider investing in a promising start-up business. *Warning:* Don't consider it unless you're entrepreneurial and excited about elevating a job into a lifestyle. Holding down a job is tough enough these days, but running and owning a business brings bigger headaches. Even more important, don't seriously consider this route until you've exhaustively checked out the company by investigating its founder, products, finances, and more. Speak to entrepreneurs who've been burned by hasty investments. They'll tell you there is no middle ground; it either works or it's a disaster.

Locating Incubators

The following organizations can point you to incubators in your state:

- National Business Incubation Association (NBIA). This membership association includes more than 500 small business incubators.
- U.S. Small Business Administration's (SBA) Office of Private Sector Initiatives, 1441 L Street NW, Suite 720A, Washington, D.C. 20416. A national clearinghouse on small business incubators, this office maintains a database of incubator projects throughout the country. Also contact your local SBA district office for information on incubator facilities in your community.

- Corporation for Enterprise Development, 777 North Capital Street NE, Suite 801, Washington, D.C. 20002. CFED promotes economic development for low-income communities.

Research Parks

Older cousins to incubators are research parks, which are managed by universities throughout the United States. Whereas incubators house different technologies under one roof, research parks are tied to technologies that the sponsoring university is developing. Most of the companies housed in research parks are midsize and large.

Companies located in research parks can utilize the university's facilities, faculty, and student body. Approximately 210,000 people work for 2800 companies located in research parks in the United States.

Finding Research Parks

Call local universities to find out if any research parks are located near you. Employ the same strategy used to find out about incubator tenants. This time, the person who holds the key to information about tenants is the park manager.

Enterprise Zones Strategy for the Hearty

Don't pursue enterprise zones unless you have a frontier spirit. They're not for everyone. Started in the early 1980s, enterprise zones are geographic areas in which tax relief, regulatory relief, and/or income incentives are offered to businesses meeting investment and job creation criteria. Enterprise zones were created to rejuvenate dying neighborhoods and communities. What better way to do it than by bringing businesses into these decaying areas?

All states require candidate zones to meet certain economic distress requirements such as high unemployment, population loss, or a high level of low-income residents. *Fact:* Enterprise zones create businesses and jobs.

While enterprise zones all differ, most are in depressed neighborhoods where crime is rampant. No late-night strolls in these neighborhoods. Business owners face an uphill battle. Success rests on having a pioneer mentality. But the rewards are worth sweating it out. You're not just launching a business, you're also revitalizing a neighborhood.

A U.S. Small Business Administration study reported that businesses with fewer than 100 employees emerged as the most important source of job growth in enterprise zones.

Evaluating Enterprise Zones What to Look For

A call to a local economic development organization will tell you if any enterprise zones are nearby. Some encompass a few blocks, others are spread out over an entire neighborhood. Baltimore, MD's zone is confined to 40 acres, while the Louisville, KY, enterprise zone encompasses over 6 square miles. Yet they both share similar goals. The goal of the Baltimore enterprise zone is to create 1750 new jobs for local residents, thereby boosting the local economy. In the Louisville zone, at least 50 percent of the employees of each business must perform almost all their services within the zone, and at least 25 percent of the employees must be zone residents.

STRATEGY: Find out what businesses are located in the zone along with the zone's objectives. Contact businesses with strong job prospects.

Small Business Development Centers

Small business development centers (SBDCs) also offer fertile job leads. The best part is they're easy to find. SBDCs provide management assistance to current and prospective small business owners.

The good news is there are 55 SBDCs—one or more in each of the 50 states, the District of Columbia, Puerto Rico, and the Virgin Islands—with a network of more than 700 branch locations. Each state has a "lead" organization which sponsors the SBDC, manages the program, and coordinates program services offered to small businesses through a network of subcenters and satellite locations. Subcenters are located at colleges, universities, community colleges, vocational schools, chambers of commerce, and economic development corporations.

Services provided by SBDCs include financial, marketing, production, organization, engineering, and technical problem and feasibility studies. Special programs and economic development activities include international trade assistance, technical assistance, procurement assistance, venture capital formation, and rural development.

Hooking Up with a Potential Employer
A Little Sleuth Work Pays Off

SBDCs are interesting, but how can they produce job leads? Simple. Your prospective boss may be taking advantage of SBDC services. Large and midsize companies are not likely to use SBDCs, but start-ups and young companies use them every day. They're all there to get help and guidance. Put it all together and it doesn't take a genius to conclude that companies seeking SBDC help could use you. You could be the smart, energetic person they're looking for.

STRATEGY: Find out who's taking advantage of a nearby SBDC. What does the company do? What financial shape is it in? How many people does it employ? What skills does it need? The person who can provide this information is the SBDC director, an associate, or a part-time volunteer worker. The director is in the people-helping business and should be more than happy to answer some, if not all, of your questions. A tactful approach is to write the SBDC director and follow up with a phone call.

55 SBDCs

Below is a list of 55 SBDCs throughout the United States.

1. University of Alabama, Birmingham, AL
2. University of Alaska/Anchorage, Anchorage, AK
3. University of Arkansas, Little Rock, AR
4. Western International University, Phoenix, AZ
5. Department of Commerce, Sacramento, CA
6. Office of Business Development, Denver, CO
7. University of Connecticut, Storrs, CT
8. Howard University, Washington, DC
9. University of Delaware, Newark, DE
10. University of Georgia, Athens, GA
11. University of Hawaii, Hilo, HI
12. Iowa State University, Ames, IA
13. Boise State University, Boise, ID
14. Department of Commerce and Community Affairs, Springfield, IL
15. Economic Development Council, Indianapolis, IN
16. Wichita State University, Wichita, KS
17. University of Kentucky, Lexington, KY
18. Northeast Louisiana University, Monroe, LA
19. University of Massachusetts, Amherst, MA
20. Department of Economic and Employment Development, Baltimore, MD
21. University of Southern Maine, Portland, ME
22. Wayne State University, Detroit, MI
23. Department of Trade and Economic Development, St. Paul, MN
24. University of Missouri, Columbia, MO
25. University of Mississippi, University, MS
26. Department of Commerce, Helena, MT
27. University of North Carolina, Raleigh, NC
28. University of North Dakota, Grand Forks, ND
29. University of Nebraska, Omaha, NE

30. University of New Hampshire, Durham, NH
31. Rutgers University, Newark, NJ
32. Santa Fe Community College, Santa Fe, NM
33. University of Nevada, Reno, NV
34. State University of New York, Albany, NY (2 locations)
35. Department of Development, Columbus, OH
36. S.E. Oklahoma State University, Durant, OK
37. Lane Community College, Eugene, OR
38. University of Pennsylvania, Philadelphia, PA
39. University of Puerto Rico, Mayaguez, PR
40. Bryant College, Springfield, RI
41. University of South Carolina, Columbia, SC
42. University of South Dakota, Vermilion, SD
43. Memphis State University, Memphis, TN
44. Dallas Community College, Dallas, TX
45. University of Houston, Houston, TX
46. Texas Tech University, Lubbock, TX
47. University of Texas, San Antonio, TX
48. University of Utah, Salt Lake City, UT
49. Department of Economic Development, Richmond, VA
50. University of Vermont, Williston, VT
51. University of the Virgin Islands, St. Thomas, USVI
52. Washington State University, Pullman, WA
53. University of Wisconsin, Madison, WI
54. Governor's Office of Community and Industrial Development, Charleston, WV
55. Casper Community College, Casper, WY

Entrepreneurial Centers

Last, but not least, check out entrepreneurial centers. SBDCs are not the only place business owners tap for affordable professional information. With the surge of business start-ups following massive dowsizings and reorganizations, entrepreneurial centers have been popping up all over the country to give budding entrepreneurs cutting-edge information. More than 300 colleges have started teaching some variation of the entrepreneurial curriculum, running the gamut from courses, lectures, seminars, and workshops to degree programs. The University of Southern California, for example, boasts a comprehensive program that started in 1971. Harvard, Wharton, Wichita State, St. Louis University, University of Arizona, Indiana University, New York University, and a slew of smaller schools offer entrepreneurial programs.

STRATEGY: Many entrepreneurs are not only taking courses, but giving them as well. Find out who these entrepreneurs are, what kinds of companies they're running, and (you guessed it) whether they may need a talented person like you to help fatten their bottom line.

The gatekeeper is the entrepreneurial director. Typically, these directors are entrepreneurial types, well-connected and happy to help. They may even provide information about the business community as well. No matter how you look at, it pays to have them in your network.

Let's move on and get the true scoop on job hopping, the survival strategy for the millennium.

CHAPTER 14

JOB HOPPING IS THE NAME OF THE GAME

RULE 14 Job hoppers get the best jobs.

If my Uncle Lewey had lived into the 1990s, he would have achieved well-earned respect. Unfortunately, neither he nor any other member of my family appreciated the fact that he was ahead of his time. Everyone called him a rootless wanderer because he changed jobs every couple of years. He was a job hopper before the term became popular.

Don't think for a moment Lewey was an unhappy man. He was a first-rate car salesman who worked for more than 20 top New York dealerships. He loved his work. He was a natural when it came to selling cars. Cars were his passion. He loved driving them, selling them, and repairing them. But he also had a sixth sense about buying trends and that's why he changed dealerships so often.

When the Volkswagen Beetle took off in the early 1960s, Lewey was in the thick of things selling a half-dozen a week. When the trend petered out, he sold American muscle cars until small cars became the rage. Lewey had a knack for being in step with the times.

Every time he changed jobs, he earned more money. Unlike his friends, Lewey made no bones about not being a company man. He didn't want to plant corporate roots and didn't think much of sticking around for a pension and retirement package. He felt that meant selling out. By staying in one place, you risk getting stale and losing your momentum. Lewey didn't intend to fall into that moat. He stayed razor-sharp by changing jobs when opportunity knocked.

Lewey was loyal to only one person: himself. He wasn't ashamed to admit it either.

Companies Want Hired Guns

Twenty years ago, Lewey was considered a contrarian and nonconformist. Today, he'd fit right in. His strategy would be applauded rather than criticized. Employers prize workers like Lewey. They appreciate their feisty, independent attitude. But most of all, they know these types love what they do and are not about to settle for something that doesn't meet their high standards.

In short, employers go out of their way to find free-thinking hired guns like Lewey. They admire the fact that they've built impressive track records through job hopping. To do so successfully means believing in yourself, taking chances, and having the guts to test the unknown.

FACT: The ideal worker is no longer someone who's logged in 15 to 20 years with one company, but someone who's been in the trenches with five to eight impressive job notches on his or her belt.

The Silicon Valley Model

In California's fast-paced Silicon Valley, job hopping has been elevated to a lifestyle. Typically, careers here are migratory, and job hopping is rewarded as an ambitious means of keeping pace with the trendy computer industry. In fact, workers who have built formidable reputations as job hoppers are much sought after by the Valley's major players. One such job-hopping legend held prestigious jobs as a computer programmer at National Semiconductor Corporation, Apple Computer, Starstuck, and Chips and Technologies. He calls himself a "start-up junkie" because he had the good sense to work for these major players during their first years in business. He was right. Each of these companies rapidly became major players in Silicon Valley's fiercely competitive computer industry.

This man is one of thousands of smart career builders who are using job hopping as a technique to ratchet themselves up to bigger and better jobs. Every industry boasts seasoned professionals like him who strategically position themselves by changing jobs often. However, there is more to job hopping than most people realize.

Three Secrets of Job Hopping

CAUTION: Not all job hoppers succeed. Constructive job hopping takes thought and planning so you're achieving your goal of moving forward. Do it badly and you'll move laterally or backward, either of which is not recommended. Ponder these three secrets of successful job hopping.

1. *Make strategic moves within the same industry.* Contrary to myth, successful job hoppers are focused and targeted. They know what they want and go after it. Each job change can be likened to a move on a chessboard. It's a carefully planned logical move, rather than an impetuous or thoughtless act. The worst kind of job hopping is either moving recklessly within your industry for a few dollars more or jumping back and forth between a few industries. Rather than building a career, all you're doing is getting some short-term rewards.
2. *Don't burn bridges.* Farsighted job hunters change jobs without leaving a bad taste in the mouths of previous employers. A take-this-job-and-shove-it attitude is career suicide. Even if you hate everything about the job—boss, colleagues, products, you name it—leave on good terms and swallow your feelings. Take the advice of thousands of job seekers who've blown their stacks for a moment of short-lived revenge. Yes, you get even by telling your boss where to go, but he or she wins in the long run. Every industry, regardless of size, boasts a powerful grapevine. Bosses talk to

one another. When word gets out that you are a loose cannon with a temper, your career prospects will suddenly not be as bright as you thought they would be. Unless you plan on changing careers or moving out of the country, getting even isn't worth it. The idea is to leave with good references.

FACT: The bigger the job and the higher you get, the more important the references.

3. *Leave in style.* That means no surprises. Give plenty of warning so the powers-that-be have plenty of time to find a replacement. Waiting the obligatory 2 weeks before telling your boss is bad form. The same goes for colleagues. Prudent job changers leave a job even better than they found it. They do everything they can to ensure a smooth transition. It starts with a carefully worded resignation letter to your boss, spelling out why you're leaving and thanking him or her for the opportunity to hone your skills. This is when diplomacy yields big rewards. Prior to telling your boss, you should alert colleagues who work closely with you. These are people you're going to be speaking to often. They're going to be your eyes and ears, telling you what's happening at the company. Naturally, once you're comfortably situated in a new company, you'll do the same thing for them.

   REMEMBER: You're part of a close-knit industry, in which not making enemies is important. Who's to say you won't wind up working for this company again or possibly doing some consulting work for it? All the more reason that it's important to make a graceful exit.

It all falls under the heading of smart networking. Successful job changers are masterful networkers. Each time they initiate a successful job change, they strengthen their network. They tighten the ties with the people they left and, at the same time, forge new relationships in their new job.

A study of 400 unemployed engineers from Brigham Young University School of Management revealed that 42 percent found work through personal contacts. It's yet another compelling statistic proving that networking pays off. Keep this in mind the next time you're thinking about changing jobs.

ADVICE

Think twice before changing jobs. Ask yourself the following questions: Why are you changing jobs? Is there any possibility of staying where you are and improving your situation? What are the benefits of the change? Once you've decided to move, lay out a strategy that guarantees a graceful transition so you don't burn any bridges.

Now, let's rock on and find out about the wonderful world of temporary employment.

CHAPTER 15

TEMPING AIN'T WHAT IT USED TO BE

Temping is a proven tactic for checking out the job landscape.

FACT: Americans are increasingly finding permanent employment through temporary service firms. Approximately 5 million temporary workers move into permanent positions each year. That's a conservative estimate, according to the National Association of Temporary and Staffing Services (NATSS), the trade association representing temp firms throughout the United States.

These are startling numbers when you consider the fact that hardly 15 years ago, temping was considered embarrassing bottom-of-the-barrel work. If you couldn't pay your rent or were deep in debt, you used a temporary service firm to get you any job that would bring in cash. Typically, the jobs were low-level clerical, maintenance, and back-office jobs.

The New Temp Game

Today, temping is a whole other ballgame. Yes, temp firms still have plenty of low-level jobs, but the great news is temping has climbed from the secretarial pool to the executive suite. In 1995, 4.8 percent of the $24.7 billion paid to temporary workers went to professionals, compared with 2.4 percent in 1991. Who would have thought professionals, ranging from attorneys, doctors, computer scientists, and accountants to journalists and senior executives, would be using temp firms? A spokesperson for Co-Counsel, a Houston-based temporary staffing firm placing attorneys and paralegals, says that contract attorneys, once shunned by mainstream legal firms, have quadrupled in the last 2 years to 40,000. Interim Services Inc., a temporary staffing company in Fort Lauderdale that specializes in commercial and health-care assignments, reports that the number of primary-care physicians working in temporary positions nationwide has increased 10 to 15 percent a year since 1990. Business is booming for TeamAlliance, a technical staffing company in New York City, providing technical professionals for short-term assignments. The company reports it's a seller's market, with applicants pulling down $75,000 to $150,000 a year, depending on skill level. In less than 2 years, TeamAlliance's sales have jumped from $1.5 million to $10 million.

Demand is also increasing for executives to fill temporary assignments. *Executive Recruiter News* (*ERN*), a newsletter covering the executive search industry, identified over 200 multimillion-dollar firms placing executive temporaries (also called "interim managers" or "flex-execs"). *ERN* publisher Jim Kennedy is bullish about this growing market for the following reasons:

- More firms are offering temp exec placement services.
- More executives at all levels are pursuing temp work.
- More companies, downsized to the limit, need interim execs for caretaker management (to cover open positions), restructuring, mentoring, and, perhaps the biggest area, special projects.
- Professional-level temps will earn more than $1 billion this year, and placement firms will generate about $100 million in fees for placing them.
- Since 1990, the number of firms serving this market has grown from 40 to 205.
- Most firms entering temp exec placement in the past 4 years have stayed with this area and most experts see it as a long-term growth trend.

For information about executive temporary jobs, pick up a copy of Kennedy's *Directory of Executive Temporary Placement Firms.*

For information, write Kennedy Publications, Templeton Road, Fitzwilliam, NH 03447.

Similar specialty temp firms in virtually all high-demand areas are reaping the benefits of the mounting need for temporary professionals.

Whaddaya Mean Temporary?

The common perception is that temporary work involves short-term assignments ranging from 2 or 3 days to a couple of months. I bet you didn't know that plenty of temp assignments can last 1 to 3 years. In fact, a temporary job can be more secure than many permanent full-time positions.

Why Hire a Temp?

Answer: It's good business. The command words for the remainder of the 1990s are "lean and mean." Don't think for a moment downsizing is over. The cutbacks will continue. What better proof than AT&T's laying off 40,000 workers in January 1996. In one fell swoop, the telecommunications giant reduced its workforce by 13 percent—and there's more to come. *Scary fact:* Since 1986, IBM has laid off more than 152,000 workers. Amazingly, Big Blue never once used the word "layoff."

As companies continue to pare staffs, temp companies meet short-term needs by supplying workers with virtually all skills. Thanks to temp firms, companies can sidestep long-term hiring commitments. As a result, prudent employers are hiring workers the same way they purchase inventory—on a just-in-time basis. They're paying for what they need when they need it, without being burdened with the cost of benefits, pension/profit-sharing plans, and medical coverage. It's pure bottom-line thinking in which all participants win. Companies instantly and cost-effectively find talent, and workers are well paid for their talents.

It's no wonder the temp industry is a $25 billion business with the temp workforce growing 10 times as fast as the permanent labor pool. About 1 in every 109 jobs is a temp position.

What Makes You Think a Full-Time Job Is So Great?

As the range of temp positions increases and the demand for temp services escalates, a new class of workers is gaining prominence. Call them professional or career temps. NATSS estimates that 39 percent of all professionals in temporary jobs prefer them to permanent positions. Dumped from secure companies, they're professionals who have discovered that temping is more fun, secure, and profitable than full-time positions. They've turned their backs on the paycheck culture and opted for a life of temping. They can stop and start work whenever they please and find work in most major cities. Computer professionals, for example, can leave frigid East Coast cities and take a 3-month assignment in western and southern cities.

ADVICE

If you're looking for excitement and enjoy testing out new jobs and meeting new people, permanent temping can be a wonderful experience. If you're in a high-demand field such as technology, medical care, business, or financial services, you can work anywhere.

Realizing their greatest assets are their people, temp firm owners make temping as attractive as possible for their workers. Along with competitive pay, many of the established players offer training options, health insurance at discounted rates, vacation pay, profit sharing, and referral bonuses. Adia Personnel, a 600-office firm, for example, gives its workers $200 in vacation pay after working 1500 hours and $400 after 2000 hours. Greenwich, CT-based Advantage, Inc., a much smaller temp firm, offers a profit-sharing plan for its employees who have completed 1000 hours of work.

Four Reasons That Temping Pays

Here's why temping makes sense.

1. *It's a wonderful morale booster.* Even if you're not hard-pressed for money, there are psychological rewards to working at many jobs until you find something you love. Rather than staying home waiting for the phone to ring, you're out in the work world mingling with people.
2. *It keeps you up to speed.* Beyond the psychological value of working steadily, there are the practical reasons that you stay current. Since temp jobs are easier to get than permanent ones, there is no better way to keep up with the latest technological bells and whistles.
3. *It's a custom-made networking platform.* Clever job searchers make the most of the opportunity. Temping allows you to earn money and shop the market by testing jobs and meeting new people. In a NATSS survey of 2508 temp workers, 54 percent of respondents said they were asked to continue on a full-time basis for the company in which they were assigned.
4. *It permits job hopping.* Think of temping as accelerated job hopping. Temp firms say the most marketable candidates are ones who've worked for a variety of businesses. This is why temp firms encourage their workers to register with several temp companies. The more notches on your experience belt, the better your chances of working steadily.

But Whom Do I Work For? How Do Temp Firms Work Anyway?

As popular as temp firms are, most people have no idea how they work. The biggest mistake is confusing them with employment agencies, a point of consternation for temp firm owners.

Employment agencies pair workers with companies and take a fee, which is a percentage of the applicant's first-year salary. Once the applicant is placed, the relationship with the employment agency ends. This contrasts with temp firms, in which the applicant's relationship is ongoing. Even though you work at an assigned location, you are paid by the temp firm (which is your employer). Most people unfamiliar with temp firms think they're paid by the client. Temp firms earn their money through commissions, which are a markup on workers' hourly wages. Depending on skill level, a markup can range from 20 to 35 percent. Accountants, paralegals, and software engineers, for example, earn more than secretaries and stenographers. Plenty of temps pull down between $20 and $35 an hour, and more.

Top Players

Below is a list of the superstars, the 36 biggest-grossing temp firms in the United States (ranked by net income, starting with the biggest producer).

36 Top Temp Firms in the United States

1. Manpower, Inc.
2. Olsten Corporation
3. Kelly Services Inc.
4. Adia Services Inc.
5. Robert Half International Inc.
6. CDI Corp.
7. Keane Inc.
8. Interim Services Inc.
9. Norell Corp.
10. Watsco Inc.
11. Computer Horizons Corp.
12. Right Management Consultants Inc.
13. Brandon Systems Corporation
14. Alternative Resources Corp.
15. Computer Task Group Inc.
16. On Assignment Inc.

17. Staff Builders Inc.
18. Careerstaff Unlimited Inc.
19. Uniforce Temporary Personnel Inc.
20. Barrett Business Services Inc.
21. National TechTeam Inc.
22. Butler International Inc.
23. Hooper Holmes Inc.
24. RCM Technologies Inc.
25. C. H. Heist Corp.
26. Personnel Management Inc.
27. Labor Ready Inc.
28. Winston Resources Inc.
29. General Employment Enterprises Inc.
30. Star Multi Care Services
31. Digital Solutions Inc.
32. Joule Inc.
33. GTS Duratek Inc.
34. Employee Solutions Inc.
35. Of Counsel Enterprises Inc.
36. Hospital Staffing Inc.

The Underside of Temping
Watch Out for Unscrupulous Outfits

The temp industry has come a long way. But, like any business, it has its fair share of shady players—quick-buck operators and con artist tin men.

Some temp firms operate like real estate agencies. Fast-talking salespeople who promise more than they can deliver practically pounce on you as soon as you walk through the door. They'll guarantee work in blue-chip firms without having the assignments to back up these promises.

Aboveboard firms put everything on the table and don't make promises they can't keep. That ranges from naming clients to explaining job functions and pay. An ethical firm pays you on a weekly or biweekly basis, and like workers employed in permanent positions, you'll receive a W-2 form rather than a 1099 form for independent contractors or consultants. A W-2 form means you're entitled to workers' compensation and unemployment insurance. A 1099 implies a consulting-type relationship which means you'll be paid when the client pays its bill. That means a few weeks or a month after completing your assignment. If you don't receive a W-2 form, make a speedy exit. It's a fraudulent temp firm that's violating the federal wage and hour law.

ADVICE

Trust your instincts. Your first clue to a bogus firm is a dingy-looking makeshift office with furniture that looks like it was picked up off the street. If the staff is poorly dressed and is rude or condescending, head for the door. In successful firms, the vibes are good—the office is cheerful and looks upscale, and the staff is polite, accommodating, and delighted to have your business.

Avoid problems by getting answers to the following questions:

1. What is the nature of the assignment?
2. How long will it last?
3. What is the hourly pay?
4. When will you be paid?
5. Will you receive a W-2 form?
6. Are there any benefits?

Finally, get your working arrangements in writing. Only an illegitimate firm will balk at that request.

Finding Temp Firms

The most efficient way to locate firms is by checking the Yellow Pages under "Employment Contractors." Call a half-dozen firms and find out what industries they service and whether they have assignments for your skill.

STRATEGY: Register with a handful of temp firms so you better your chances of getting assignments.

It's time to speed up the tempo and prepare for interviews. The first step is dumping the résumé and finding a better tool for attracting employers' attention.

CHAPTER 16

TRASH YOUR RÉSUMÉ

Abandon the résumé and craft a well-written letter that is both résumé and cover letter in an all-in-one targeted package.

Dump the résumé! What kind of outrageous chutzpah is that? I might as well be defiling motherhood, the American flag, Ronald McDonald, and Coca-Cola in one fell swoop. Exile this guy to another galaxy pronto.

Hold on. Before you charge back to the bookstore to demand a refund, give me a chance to make my case. First, imagine you're running a big company and you received the résumés of R. David Thomas, Al Copeland, and Richard Branson, the founders, respectively, of Wendy's, Popeye's and Virgin Atlantic Airlines. But assume you didn't know they were entrepreneurial superstars. I could just imagine your reaction. Start with Thomas. Your reaction would be like this: "This guy didn't even finish tenth grade; he moved around the country working in restaurants, hooked up with Colonel Parker of Kentucky Fried Chicken (KFC), and ran a couple of KFCs before starting his own fast-food chain. I don't see any solid management experience, just a bunch of low-level restaurant jobs."

You'd react the same way to Copeland's and Branson's résumés. Both men were also high school dropouts. Before launching Popeye's fast-food chain, Copeland worked in a slew of doughnut shops and fast-food restaurants, but had no managerial experience. And

Branson? He could barely stick with any business longer than a year. He had his hands in so many pots, it's a wonder he knew what was cooking at all. So what if he launched Virgin Records, Virgin Atlantic Airlines, and a number of other multimillion-dollar businesses and he's one of the richest men in the United Kingdom? He's unstable. And his résumé stinks.

You get the idea. You'd think any company would kill to get these men on their payrolls? Not on your life.

With this said, I begin my attack on the résumé. If you wouldn't hire these men because their résumés were unimpressive, how could anyone argue that the résumé is an accurate barometer of a person's abilities? If résumés don't work for genius entrepreneurs, how could they work for the average job searcher?

Résumés Deliver Results for Only 5 Percent of Job Searchers

The truth is résumés work for about 5 percent of job searchers—and that's stretching the truth. These fortunate job hunters just happened to have perfect backgrounds. They attended blue-chip schools, held a few fast-track jobs in Fortune 500 companies, and maybe were in the right place at the right time. In addition, they remained in one industry riveted to one job track. In short, they created the impression of being consistent high-performers with no career blemishes.

That's all well and good, but how many of us fall into that elite category? Not a heck of a lot. It's human nature to stumble and make a few bad moves before finding our true calling. Yet you can't show human failing on a résumé. The human resources folks are not forgiving when it comes to evaluating credentials. They don't give a hoot about your trials and tribulations or about the bad hand life has dealt you. A corporate drone's reaction will be to promptly dispatch your résumé to the reject pile without a second thought. Unfair, you say. So what? Life isn't fair, so why should job hunting be any different?

Humorist Gene Perret summed up the résumé nicely, "About all one can tell from a résumé is that the author owns a typewriter (or computer) or knows someone who does." In *Throw Away Your Résumé* (Barron's), Robert Hochheiser goes even further. In 183 pages, Hochheiser says résumés are the "worst way to sell your services."

Heed the advice of Jim Challenger, respected career expert and president of Chicago outplacement firm Challenger, Gray & Christmas:

> While still heralded as the key to winning a job, the résumé is actually today's number-one deterrent to getting a job. Many rely on the résumé as an almost sacred tool and expect it to do everything for them in the job search. It never did and never will, especially now, with large numbers of job-seekers competing for far fewer jobs.

"Hiring a worker from a résumé is like trying to hire a ballplayer from his bubblegum card," adds Perret.

Résumé Madness
So Why Do We Persist in Writing Résumés?

There are two big reasons we keep on churning out résumés. First, old habits are hard to break. For almost half a century résumés produced interviews. What happened? It's as simple as the world changed. Blame it on technology, international competition, and the emergence of the global market. The United States, once the world industrial power, found itself dueling with mighty foes like Japan, the Pacific Rim countries, and, to a lesser extent, Western and Eastern Europe. All of a sudden, we were fighting off competitors who could turn out products, from cars to computers, not only more cheaply than American-made goods, but often better. It didn't take a management consultant to tell companies what needed to be done. It was either pare costs and make better products or perish. Before companies could clean up their acts, the first order of business was figuring out how to make better widgets economically. For starters, they learned it could be done with fewer people. So they fired folks like you and me. There you have it. The result is a classic economic dilemma: The supply of workers far exceeds the number of jobs available. Hence, corporations suddenly found themselves sinking in résumés.

The second reason we keep churning out résumés is we've been brainwashed. Again, blame industry. Despite fewer jobs, companies still demand résumés. When they need a body, they clamor for résumés. That's the way they hired in the past, so why break tradition?

It's no wonder job hunters still think résumés are job conduits. If they only knew they were fighting against treacherous odds.

A Smart Monkey Can Write a Great Résumé
The Big-Buck Résumé Business

Plenty of folks are getting rich off résumés. In a strategic corner with a bird's-eye view of the job market, is the profit-hungry publishing industry, which keeps turning out résumé books with machinelike efficiency.

About 75 résumé books are on the market, with some 25 to 30 more in the works. Every major publisher has at least one résumé book on store shelves. Publishers work hard to hook readers on catchy titles like *Knock 'Em Dead Résumés!* Is one book strikingly different from the next? Absolutely not! How many ways can anyone explain the difference between a chronological and functional résumé? Or how many different ways can you write a cover letter? A smart monkey can be trained to write a résumé.

If you don't want to go the old-fashioned route and buy a résumé book, there's plenty of résumé-writing software available. There are a couple of dozen packages on the market at this very moment. Just boot up your computer, click the mouse on the right icon, punch in the appropriate information, and voilà, instant résumé. Like all computer products, résumé software can be purchased at bargain prices. It's hard to resist the enticing promotional programs hawking the stuff. One ad from a New York daily said, "Résumé anxiety put to rest. If the thought of writing a résumé causes you more anxiety than filling out a college application form, there's good news: There is a new software program to help. Expert Software's *Expert Résumé-Writer for Windows* ($11.99) contains 100 sample résumés and 12 résumé templates. There are also some sample cover letters and an appointment calendar." It's a wonder they don't throw in a year's subscription to *Playboy* (or *Playgirl*) as an added inducement.

The last option is to hire a professional résumé writer. You can actually earn a living writing résumés! There's even a Professional Association of Résumé Writers (PARW) in St. Petersburg, FL. If this keeps up, colleges will be handing out bachelor's degrees in résumé writing. We'll be in big trouble if that happens.

A résumé-writing service in Kansas charges clients as much as $1000 to write a résumé. For an additional charge, they'll mass-market it to potential employers in a database of 10 million names. One desperate job searcher spent $8000 to send out 10,000 résumés to companies all over the United States. The pathetic results: 14 interviews and no job. Meanwhile, the résumé company is pulling down a few million dollars a year.

Mass-mailing résumés has created the term "junk résumé." Like junk mail, it's discarded immediately. Outplacement specialist Challenger warns against mass-mailing résumés. He estimates only a 1 to 2 percent return, making it an expensive waste of time.

The résumé madness doesn't stop there. Not content with using the U.S. Postal Service, aggressive job hunters are also faxing their résumés. Mistakenly, they think it's the fastest way to get their résumés into employers' hands. If they only knew that overburdened employers trash them as soon as they pop out of the machine. Frustrated business owners stop them in their tracks by pulling the plug on their fax machines.

Still others, who've tried the above approaches, are sending résumés electronically. They call it "electronic networking." There are even a few books out on preparing electronic résumés. One such title is *Electronic Résumés for the New Job Market* (*Résumés That Work 24 Hours a Day*). It tells you how to prepare an electronic résumé so it's easily read by a computer. The idea is to write a résumé that can be incorporated into a job bank available to employers searching for job candidates. The new twist is learning which key words the computer will look for and then incorporating them into your résumé.

While it sounds very high-tech and sophisticated, don't think it gives you a leg up on your competition. The electronic résumé is the newest job-hunting gimmick.

"The Envelope, Please"

With all this sophisticated technology, you'd think we'd get some award-winning résumés. Not so. The result is what I call the, "generic" or "white bread" résumé. It's a mediocre and uninspired résumé that looks the same as everyone else's. In a word, it's downright boring. All of these résumés use the same tired buzzwords (implemented, impacted, growth-oriented, maximize, utilized, etc.), and even the same fonts, layout, and paper.

The Résumé Dilemma
"I Bet I Can Read a Résumé Faster Than You Can!"

The result is that all these mediocre résumés are driving human resources people to drink. Overburdened résumé readers are pulling out their hair trying to find résumés that stand out. It's no wonder speed-reading résumés is practically a sport. Human resources folks joke about how little time they spend reading résumés. One staffing manager of a Silicon Valley company says he spends no more than 30 seconds scanning a résumé. If he spots something that catches his eye, he might spend as much as a whole minute reading it. He adds that high-quality résumés are the exception, not the rule. Most employers and managers say they spend under a minute reading each résumé.

That's easy to understand when you consider the truckload of résumés some companies receive each year. Fortune 500 companies the likes of IBM and AT&T, for example, receive over 1 million résumés a year. Computer companies such as Microsoft and Sun Microsystems receive close to 3000 résumés a week. Robert Half, head of an international recruiting firm and author of several career books, said that if 1000 personnel executives did nothing but read all the résumés in circulation, it would take an average of 71 years, figuring 4 minutes per résumé. Half contends that if these résumés were laid out end to end, they would encircle the earth 15 times. That's a frightening reality.

Will the Résumé Madness Ever End? Please Tell Me the Solution

One thing is certain: old habits don't change quickly. Think of the resistance Christopher Columbus encountered. After a couple of centuries of thinking the world is flat, along comes some lunatic insisting it's round. A lot of intelligent people swore that if you sailed too far, you'd fall off the end of the earth. So it's no surprise job hunters feel secure churning out résumés the way they've always done.

Put it all together and there aren't too many people telling you résumés don't work. It's not like career experts are giving you the straight poop and trying to wean you off the résumé habit. So don't beat yourself up if you've been following the crowd. It's never too late to try something new.

If you're saying to yourself, "There's got to be a better way to capture interviews," you're right.

The inevitable question: If résumés don't work, what does? *Answer:* a simple letter.

Send a Letter Instead of a Résumé? "Ah Come On, You Can't Be Serious!"

I couldn't be more serious. The beauty lies in its simplicity and elegance. Times change, yet some things remain the same. One of them is the universal appreciation of a well-written letter. Employers love rule breakers. The trick is breaking the rules with panache, taste, and professionalism. A well-conceived letter fits the bill perfectly.

Is it foolproof? Absolutely not. There are no guarantees a letter will get you interviews. One thing is certain: You stand a better chance of capturing attention with a letter than you do with your résumé. For that reason alone, it's a worth a try. You have nothing to lose, everything to gain.

Don't think a great letter is easy to write though. Anyone can turn out a résumé in an hour or two. But a letter requires more effort and thought. There are no formulas, shortcuts, or press-and-click software programs that will make the job easier. *You've* got to make it great. There lies the challenge and motivation to craft a superior product.

Here's why a letter fits the bill.

Three Reasons a Letter Beats a Résumé

1. It's a one-of-a-kind personal statement. There is no better way to stand out from the crowd and get noticed. By now, you must have figured out that marching to the same beat as everyone else isn't going to get you very far.
2. It's a complete package, replacing résumé and cover letter.
3. It's ideal for all job hunters, but especially job hoppers, career changers, and people who haven't worked for lengthy periods (such as mothers returning to the workforce).

A résumé is little more than a listing of jobs, whereas a letter allows you to explain frequent job changes. It's a platform to sell yourself. Take the woman who took a 4-year maternity leave. On a résumé, the 4-year gap looks suspicious, but a letter permits you to justify how you made good use of the time. An employer might read it and conclude, "I admire this woman for interrupting her career to be with her child. I also like the fact that she freelanced during her leave of absence."

A letter is also a perfect vehicle for career changers. Imagine spending 20 years working as an accountant and then trying to get a job as a computer programmer. What does it matter if you're a fanatical hobbyist hacker and technowhiz. It will look odd on a résumé. "What's with this guy? One day he's an accountant, the next he's a programmer." Immediately, you're cast as a rootless dabbler. A letter permits you to make an eloquent case for the change. A sentence like this makes the change seem perfectly natural: "I loved accounting, but as the field became more technological and we started incorporating computer software into our practices, the technology side fascinated me more than the accounting side. Over a 5-year period I took MIS courses followed by several programming courses and got to the point where I could design my own computer programs. I now want to segue from accounting to programming and eventually software design." How would you feel after reading this? I bet you'd say to yourself, "I like the way this guy carefully planned the change and made the move when he was ready. I admire him for having the guts to change direction and do something he loves."

Hundreds of similar stories can be cited. When all is said and done, a letter can be molded to sell *all* job hunters, no matter how unconventional the background. But it's up to you write a dynamite letter. I'm going to show you how.

What's a Great Letter and What Should It Say?

First, some warnings. A letter should never be preachy, long-winded, or too familiar. It should never read like an autobiography. It must be concise, tightly written, and no longer than one and a half pages. If it runs more than two pages, it may not be read. Brevity is the key.

The tone ought to be respectful, sincere, upbeat, and professional.

REMEMBER: There is a big difference between a personal and a professional letter. In a personal letter you can say anything you want, breaking all the rules of grammar and good taste. You can be abrupt, rude, and crude. You can employ sentence fragments, colloquialisms, and slang to your heart's content.

It's a whole different story with professional letters. You can be honest and direct, yet the letter must fall within traditional bounds. You must use clear, concise, conversational English and avoid anything possibly in bad taste. The goal is to make an instant connection by being tactful and professional. Uppermost, the content must provoke immediate interest.

Think of a great letter as a cross between a good news story and an enticing print ad. Both beg to be read by whetting the reader's appetite in the opening paragraph. It must be honest, impart information, and, naturally, sell you. And there shouldn't be a wasted word in the entire letter.

If the letter achieves its goal, an employer will say, "Hey, I can't believe this woman sent me a letter instead of a résumé. But you know, it's damned good. She's got an incredible background and I like her style. Call her up and ask her to come in this Thursday."

Now let's write a killer letter.

The ABCs of Writing Mind-Blowing Letters
The Structure Is the Same, Only the Content Changes

I'm going to take the pain out of writing a letter. Think of it as crafting a flexible vehicle that can land you a job. Once the form and foundation for the letter are created, only the opening paragraphs have to be molded so they apply to the job you're after.

Before you start writing the letter, answer these two important questions:

1. What is the employer looking for? Be precise. List not only the technical and professional skills needed, but the personal ones as well.
2. What jobs in your background best sell you for this job? Again, here's where a letter beats out a résumé every time. You don't have to list every job you've held in the past decade, but do include the two or three that best sell you. And they don't have to be sequential jobs either.

Building the Letter

A great letter has three parts: introduction, development, and closing. It ought to get the reader's attention, make a promise, and back it with compelling facts. Translated, it means the first part of your letter piques the reader's interest, the second part sells you by citing relevant jobs, and the last part winds down by asking for an interview.

It's pretty straightforward, but it's how you develop these three components that will make or break the letter. Check out this sample.

December 4, 19XX

Mr. Irwin Fugicle-Slipshod
Paddy-Waddy Cookies, Ltd.
6798 South Bethune Fork
Los Angeles, CA XXXXX

Dear Mr. Fugicle-Slipshod:

Tommy LeBiano, marketing manager of Peek-a-Boo Fancy Baked Goods, suggested I contact you about the marketing manager position. I've known Tommy for 15 years since we met at Ding-a-Ling Fancy Products. He was running their yogurt division and I was the company's marketing specialist.

I've worked in the food business ever since I graduated from college. I've watched it emerge from a tiny industry made up of mom-and-pop businesses to a multibillion-dollar international industry. The change has been startling and exciting.

With all this growth, the industry has become competitive, elevating marketing to a critical function. I offer 25 years of marketing experience. I've worked in the trenches for both large and small companies.

In my last position as marketing director of Ding-Dong Doughnuts, I headed a marketing team that was responsible for cracking the South American and European markets. Over a 3-year period, these powerful markets boosted sales by 35 percent.

Prior to that, I was marketing manager of Slick Gourmet Foods, where I designed a program that placed the company's expensive line of gourmet products in 10 of the country's top supermarket chains. Before that, Slick's products were sold exclusively in gourmet and specialty shops. This strategic move doubled sales in less than 2 years.

My apprentice years were spent in sales and marketing positions at Cronos Products and Proud Mary Cookies, two small pioneer companies that changed the food industry.

These are just a few of the highlights of my career. At your convenience, I would like to sit down with you and share some insights I have about Paddy-Waddy Cookies, Ltd. With the retrenching of your archcompetitor, the once powerful Docile Doughnuts, you're well poised to pounce on markets they once controlled. I'd like to share some strategies that could help you do it.

With your company's reputation as an innovator that can move quickly, I see Docile's troubles as a blessing in disguise. With your knowledge of niche markets and the respect you've garnered from every major supermarket chain, you're ready for aggressive growth.

I hold a BA from Northeastern University and an MBA from the University of Southern California.

I've provided only a brief sketch of my background. I look forward to filling in the gaps and discussing the food industry in more detail when we meet.

During the week of December 10, I will call to arrange a mutually convenient appointment.

I look forward to meeting you.

Sincerely,

Joey Dante Infernos, Jr.

ANALYSIS: Let's take it from the top and evaluate Joey D's letter. Not wasting a moment, he hooks his reader by making an immediate connection. By opening with Tommy LeBiano's name, he's captured his reader's attention. The trick is holding it. He goes on to establish credibility by explaining the history of the relationship. The fact that they've known each other for 15 years says they're colleagues and friends. This is not a casual contact used to get a foot in the door, but someone who can be called on to get the true scoop on Joey.

Joey wastes no time in selling his credentials. He drives home the fact that he's not only a 25-year veteran of the food business but he loves what he does. So far, he's doing a bang-up job but hasn't begun to aggressively sell himself. When he does, he hits the bull's-eye immediately by avoiding hollow claims and focusing on impressive facts. "In my last position as marketing director of Ding-Dong Doughnuts, I headed a marketing team responsible for cracking the South American and European markets. Over a 3-year period these powerful markets boosted sales by 35 percent."

He goes on to reveal even more stunning credentials that would impress any prospective employer. Yet he strategically skips over trivial jobs and titles and focuses on the highlights.

He doesn't stop there. He waits until the end to say "At your convenience, I would like to sit down with you and share some insights I have about Paddy-Waddy Cookies, Ltd. With the retrenching of your archcompetitor, the once powerful Docile Doughnuts, you're poised to pounce on markets they once controlled. I'd like to share some strategies that could help you do it." Joey could be bluffing, but any employer would be foolish not to check him out.

Lastly, he's tactfully pushy when he says he intends to call "during the week of December 10."

All in all, let's give Joey high marks for writing a compelling letter that stands an excellent chance of scoring interviews. If you were an employer, would you want to see what this applicant is like? I would.

Use the above letter as your guide and mind the following letter-writing no-nos.

Five No-Nos

1. *Don't ramble.* Be terse and stay focused. Include only information that captures attention and sells you. Anything else is irrelevant. Don't lose sight of your goal: *to capture interviews.*
2. *Avoid hollow claims and empty statements.* "I'm a highly creative person who enjoys challenging problems." "I have a real talent for problem solving. I don't give up until I find solutions." Big deal. Instead, list impressive accomplishments that prove you're the best thing since pizza. The reader will draw his or her own conclusions.
3. *Do not include personal information.* Do not mention age, marital status, religion, hobbies, membership in organizations (Elks, Free Masons), or health status ("I'm in perfect health"). It's all irrelevant. Finally, skip the silly line found on the bottom of most résumés, "References furnished upon request." First, it's inappropriate. Second, if an employer is interested, are you going to refuse to provide references?
4. *Never bad-mouth a former employer.* For sure it's tempting, but it's the height of bad form. Do not say you left your last job

because your boss was a gutless moron for not backing your projects, or mention that your boss was always pawing you and saying inappropriate things. So what if it's the truth? What matters is that it makes you look bad. Even though you may have been perfectly in the right, an employer could conclude that you can't get along with others; you're not a team player and, hence, are a poor risk. In short, employers don't want to hear about personal problems. Simply sidestep controversial issues. During the interview, it's a different story. We'll get to that shortly.

5. *Do not mail a letter to a title.* One of the letter's important selling points is that it's targeted to a real person, creating an immediately favorable impression. It shows you've gone to the trouble of identifying not only a job, but also the person who's hiring for it.

Two Tips for Crafting Award-Winning Letters

1. *Be articulate and find your own voice.* Nobody wants to hire a clone. Don't try to sound like a pedant or a corpocrat by sprinkling your letter with business-speak or technospeak. That's downright annoying, not to mention a turnoff. Be articulate and use old-fashioned plain English. Use short, rather than long weighty sentences.
2. *Never go with a first draft.* Tolstoy, Shakespeare, and Hemingway would never submit a first draft. Take the hint. Don't be lazy. Put time and effort into your letters and you'll see great results.

ADVICE

Rather than constantly going over a letter until you're satisfied, put it aside for a few hours. Better yet, stash it overnight, then make changes. You'll be surprised what some distance can do. Professional writers endorse this technique. You'll be amazed at the changes you'll make when you reread it. You'll cut, tighten, and rework sentences. The result will be a stronger letter.

Tailor the Letter to the Job

Once you've perfected your letter, you can expand or contract it to fit the job for which you're applying. You don't have to create a totally new letter every time you apply for a new job. Just adapt it by adding or subtracting material. Let's say you're an engineer with a strong electronics and computer background. Over a 20-year career, for example, you've worked in both areas using similar skills. Depending on the type of firm you're writing to, highlight the most appropriate accomplishments.

Before we drop the letter in an envelope and stamp and bless it, let's take one last step. Let's make sure it's "letter"-perfect.

Last-Minute Task Letter Checklist

To be doubly sure your letter is ready, answer these four questions:

1. *How does it look?* Are there any smudges or stains on the paper? Did you allow generous margins, at least half an inch on both sides? What about unnecessary spaces?
2. *Are there any spelling errors?* Don't rely on your computer software's spell-check function. Read the letter over carefully, scrutinizing every word. *Critical:* Is the name of the person you're sending it to spelled correctly? Mangle his or her name and you've batted out before your letter is even read.
3. *How does it read?* Is it professional and businesslike rather than chatty and familiar?
4. *Does the letter focus on significant selling accomplishments?*

LAST WORD: Keep track of all letters by creating a log, which includes when and to whom each letter is sent and the status of the letter (whether it yielded positive or negative results).

If you've done a crackerjack job, you've landed an interview. Let's step into the hot seat and fire back some award-winning answers.

CHAPTER 17

LIGHTS! CAMERA! YOU'RE ON! THE INTERVIEW NIGHTMARE

RULE 17 The more time you spend preparing for an interview, the better your chances of winning a job offer.

This is it, the ultimate performance. Fortunately, you can rewrite a letter till the cows come home, but you can't replay an interview. Once you botch this scene, you can't call an employer and say, "Ms. Attila-Capone, could you give me 30 minutes of your time so I could come back and redo the interview? I've rethought all my answers and I'd like another shot at the job of pea-shooter designer. I guarantee you'll be impressed this time."

It's a great fantasy, but things don't happen this way in real life. When it comes to interviews, you don't get a second chance. Screw up and you don't get the job. The curtain falls. There are few certainties in life. This is one of them.

It's no wonder people have nightmares the night before the interview. When you get past all the rah-rah stuff you've read in career books and the advice you've received from friends, advisers, and well-wishers, there is no getting away from the unalterable fact that interviews are scary as hell.

The only thing you can do about it is the best you can. That's not trite advice either. The truth is that most job hunters don't work hard enough at mastering the interview. They merely show up and let the chips fall where they may. That's playing the game badly.

Let's start with attitude.

There's That Attitude Thing Again No-Hope-Harrys Stay Unemployed

I said it before and I'll say it again. Attitude is critical. A positive attitude is a healthy attitude. A positive attitude predisposes you to success; a negative attitude sets you up for failure. A lot of folks feel they have to suffer before they enjoy the fruits of success. It's the kind of psychological stuff that shrinks have been writing about since Adam. The barriers to performing at peak efficiency range from fear of rejection or success to low self-esteem. In short, people are often their own worst enemies.

It's no wonder they don't give 100 percent. That goes for their job search as well. Going about job hunting passively is sure to deliver dismal results. Passive job hunters are like ships without engines or sails. They bounce around waiting for the winds of change to take them where they will. If they're lucky, they'll find jobs before their teeth fall out.

If you're a "No-Hope-Harry," you won't get far. Like a lighthouse beacon, your negative attitude will be spotted miles away. It will be detected in your eyes and by your posture, your tone, and the way you carry yourself. You'll be at the whim of the world, manipulated, controlled, and inevitably discarded.

A good attitude is infectious. Every day offers another shot at the brass ring. Who knows? You could win the lottery. Regular people win it all the time. It's not that you're banking on a windfall; more important, you realize it's possible. That's a positive attitude. The same thinking applies to your job search. If you're operating with a positive mindset, every day brings renewed optimism. This could be the day bringing new leads, second interviews, maybe a job offer. Fueled by enthusiasm, you work harder and increase your chances of snatching a job.

No matter how tough things get, stay positive. Now let's put the interview in perspective.

It's Only a Performance

Think of the interview as an audition. You are the performer and the interview is your shot at a great part. Just as actors must study their lines to perform them brilliantly, you too must know what to say and how to convince the interviewer you are the *only* person for the job.

Who Is This Guy and What Does He Want? Remember Why You're There Sell! Sell! Sell!

It may make you feel better to think of the interviewer as a discerning consumer confronted with many brands of a product. Each product is wrapped differently with a different aura and feel to it. Taking this analogy to the next logical step, you must make yourself the most enticing product on the shelf. Not only must you look right, you must act right. You should appear not as an inexpensive, budget product, but as a top-of-the-line model. You're not a Ford, Chevrolet or Volkswagen, but a Rolls-Royce, Bentley, Lamborghini, or Ferrari. You have to come across like a high-performance product that appreciates, not depreciates, with age. You must be irresistible.

If that analogy doesn't work for you, equate the interview to a salesperson's cold call. Crackerjack salespeople thrive on uncertainly. They never know what they're going to encounter once they cross the threshold of a prospective client. They could be meeting a clone of Mother Teresa or a distant relative of the Marquis de Sade. But it's that uncertainly that turns them on, fires their imagination, and inspires them to give their best performance.

Apply the same thinking to an interview. Unless you have inside information on the interviewer, more likely it will be the luck of the draw. Wouldn't you be surprised if you're greeted by a person who is more afraid of you than you are of him or her? It happens every day.

Now for the interrogation.

What to Expect
All Interviews Are Different

The majority of interviews are informal one-on-one arrangements. Nevertheless, there are exceptions. Be prepared for these six interview situations.

1. *The screening interview.* It's usually brief, but the object is to find out whether you should be considered as a candidate for the job and passed on to the next interviewer. A screening interview can run from 5 to 15 minutes in length. In that brief time, the interviewer will know whether you are the type of applicant the company requires.

   If it's a much-sought-after position, it's not uncommon for the screening interview to be conducted on the phone. Keep your guard up. If the person is asking direct, pertinent questions, your answers should be equally direct and pertinent. Many of us tend to relax and assume a casual manner when speaking on the phone.
2. *The traditional interview.* This is probably the easiest type of interview, because there are no surprises. It takes the form of a casual, easygoing conversation. As the conversation progresses, questions are asked and information is imparted so the interviewer will be able to come to a decision regarding your suitability for the position.

   In the traditional interview setting, the interviewer appears tolerant and sensitive to what you have to say. The interviewer's goal is to make you feel comfortable so that you are at ease and can be fairly considered.
3. *The unstructured interview.* The unstructured interview is an entirely different situation. Instead of working to create a harmo-

nious, accepting atmosphere, the interviewer sits back and waits for you to "do your thing" and impress the hell out of him or her. For example, the interviewer may fold his or her arms, slouch back in the chair, and say, "Why don't you tell me about yourself?" Without expecting it, the ball is tossed to you and you have little choice but to run with it. If you're not prepared for this approach, it can be unnerving, to say the least. The interviewer puts no time limit on your answers and patiently waits for you to either come out victorious or hang yourself.

The unstructured interview has been compared to psychotherapy, during which the therapist does minimal talking and the patient talks nonstop. It's also been compared to a military interrogation, in which close-mouthed interrogators silently stare their captors into confessing.

If you're not prepared for it, the unstructured interview's lack of direction can result in anxiety. However, if you know your stuff and have your interview routine down pat, you'll have no problems.

4. *The group interview.* Self-explanatory. There are some sound reasons for it, but the group interview can be stressful. Some companies use it religiously as a time-saver. Instead of holding four separate interviews, for instance, you'll be interviewed by four people at once. The important thing to remember in a group interview is that you're probably going to have something to do with each person interviewing you. Let's say you're applying for the position of eastern sales manager. Since this is an important sales position, it stands to reason you'll be interviewed by the president of the company, the senior vice president in charge of sales, and one or two regional managers. Each one has an investment in getting the right person for the job. Instead of viewing the situation as intimidating, imagine that each person is conducting his or her own interview. Each person has separate interests and each question will reflect a different point of view and attitude.

   While they seem frightening, most group interview situations are relaxed and informal. Prior to the interview actually starting, for example, coffee may be served and you'll chat with the group. Who knows? You might even enjoy it.

5. *The serial interview.* Imagine the above assemblage of VPs interviewing you separately, rather than in a group setting. This is a time-consuming procedure, and naturally there will be a lot of repetition. You'll find yourself giving the same information over and over. However, work to turn in a stunning performance on each interview. Think of each session as the deciding interview, the one that's going to nail the job. This way the repetition and tedium won't bother you.
6. *The stress interview.* Don't lose any sleep over the stress interview. Typically, stress interviews are used for high-stress jobs. If you're applying for a job as air-traffic controller, private detective, bodyguard, FBI agent, or CIA investigator, you may have to undergo a stress interview. As you might guess, the interviewer goes out of his or her way to create a stressful situation by firing probing questions to determine how you react under pressure. By the time it's over, you'll be enjoying some technicolor fantasies about getting even.

   Obviously, if you're calm, cool, and collected and shoot back all the right answers, you're the person for the job. If you have a temper tantrum, scream, cry, or lose your cool and hurl the interviewer out the window, you won't get the job.

Score Points by Making Connections and Building Rapport

If you're lucky, you'll hit it off with your interviewer immediately. You'll shake hands, smile, and sense camaraderie with someone who understands you. For some unexplainable reason, you'll make an instant connection.

But don't get your hopes up. This doesn't happen all the time. More likely, you'll have to hang back and work at making a connection. Sometimes, no matter how hard you try, it just won't happen. Nevertheless, whether you're greeted by the maharishi or the ghost of serial killer Jeffrey Dahmer, be cool, take your cues from the interviewer, and do your best.

The first 5 minutes are critical, determining how the rest of the interviewer will go. These critical minutes point up the importance of first impressions. Lee Iacocca, Chrysler's savior, said in his autobiography, "I learned to figure out people pretty quickly. To this day, I can usually tell a fair amount about somebody from our first meeting."

Writer Norman King goes further. In *The First Five Minutes* (Prentice-Hall), he says: "By the time the second hand has traveled five times around your wristwatch, two things will have happened. You will have decided exactly how much you trust or distrust your business acquaintance and, likewise, the other person will have decided exactly how much he or she trusts or distrusts you."

Now that you know what to expect, let's take it from the top and go through the whole interview process. Below are four strategies for turning in an award-winning performance.

Four Strategies for Zapping Interviews

Strategy 1: Look the Part

Sorry to disappoint you, but fitting in means looking like everyone else in the corporate world. If you're a flamboyant dresser who likes to make a statement by wearing wild colors and going to all lengths to be a trendsetter, you'd best curb this impulse if you hope to get a job quickly. "Does that mean I can't be me and must look like everyone?" Afraid so. If you insist on being a rebel and dressing in rainbow plaids or Hawaiian sports shirts with wild jackets to match and a long dangling earring to show you're trendy, prepare yourself for some disappointments. Or if you're a woman who likes to do her own thing and sport tight slacks with accompanying 5-inch spike heel-pumps and wild sweaters, you too are in for a rude awakening.

Possibly, once you're employed, you can loosen up and wear more casual duds. But while you're looking for work, you had better please corporate recruiters and repressed human resources types. Dress *conservatively.* Ironically, the world changes daily and clothing fads and trends change practically every season, yet corporate styles change little from year to year. If you doubt me, gather some annual reports from major corporations that go back 20 years. Thumb through them and see how the executive corps dresses. Maybe hairstyles are longer or shorter, yet the men are still wearing two- or three-piece suits in inoffensive grays, browns, and blacks; ties are striped or solid and the tie knot is traditional Windsor. And rest assured, shoes are similarly conservative, probably black, brown, or cordovan.

And women are wearing white blouses, with accompanying gray, blue, tan, brown, or black jackets and skirts. Hair is neat and conservatively coiffed; just enough makeup is used to create a professional, confident air.

Boring, you shout! Sorry, but that's the way it is. And if corporate dress hasn't changed much in the past few decades, it's not about to change much come the millennium. It's not just American businesspeople who stick to the same style of dressing, but businesspeople worldwide. You'll notice only slight differences in dress among French, Japanese, British, Italian, Dutch, Scandinavian, and American businesspeople. It's safe to conclude that an international dress code exists in corporate circles.

There are variations, however. Some industries tend to be looser about dress than others. The fashion and entertainment industries allow workers to dress more casually. Yet everywhere else, conservative dress is the rule. And some industries, notably finance and banking, are ultraconservative, almost bordering on a funereal look. Walk into an old-line Wall Street brokerage house and you'll be startled by the majority of workers in the same uniform—dark three-button suits, vests, white or blue oxford-cloth shirts, and similarly conservative matching ties. It's almost frightening. Yet that's the uniform you'll have to wear if you intend to work in that environment.

You don't have to look like a Wall Street investment banker, but it's important you look like a seasoned professional, which again translates into sober, conservative colors. Why tempt fate? Every time you go on an interview, wear your Sunday best.

To take the pain out of dressing, below are some guidelines. First, the men.

1. *Stick to a conservative suit.* If it's fall or winter, the preferred colors are black, brown, or gray. During spring and summer you can lighten up a bit and wear cord, seersucker, or pinstripe tan and olive suits. Occasionally, you can get away with a conservative sports jacket (preferably herringbone) and a pair of dark pants. However, you'd do best sticking to suits. If in doubt, emulate the Ivy League style of dressing. Harvard, Princeton, Yale, and Dartmouth graduates all look the same from year to year. They can walk right out of school and into a Fortune 500 company and not have to change their style of dressing. If you think this look is insufferably dull and it's not you, wear it anyway. Corporate America loves it.
2. *Keep your hair short and neatly trimmed.* You don't have to look like a West Point graduate, but you should look clean-cut.
3. *Ties should be striped or solid or have a simple design.* They shouldn't be too narrow or too wide, but perfectly blended with the rest of your outfit. Nothing too wild. No purples, pinks, or metallic-looking colors.
4. *Beards and mustaches must be neatly trimmed.* Whatever you do, don't walk into an interview sporting a Rip Van Winkle beard or you'll experience the shortest interview of your career. If you have a beard, make sure it is neatly trimmed and of conservative length. Avoid a handlebar, pencil, or waxed mustache. The women may love it, but I guarantee your interviewer won't.

Now the women.

1. *Dresses or skirts and matching jackets make up the perfect corporate uniform.* Don't wear just any jacket and skirt, but a suit that is finely tailored and fits perfectly. That means it should be

neither too loose nor too snug. Make sure the skirt is neither too long nor too short. Check out some of the fashion mags to find the skirt length of the day. As for colors, women are expected to don the same color combinations as their male counterparts.

2. *Hair should be of respectable length.* That means not too short and not too long. Hair down to your waist is not appreciated. Corporate America has no fondness for freeze-dried hippies. Keep it clean, neat, and on the short side. Avoid highly stylized, dyed hairdos. Again, stay on top of the fashion mags.
3. *Wear just enough makeup.* How much is enough? Enough does not mean looking as though you are about to be photographed for a cosmetics ad or go on stage for a Broadway production. Enough makeup highlights your good features and plays down your poor ones. Let discretion and common sense guide you.

Finally, carry an attaché case with you on every interview. It's a recommended prop. Not a beaten-up, worn leather case that's been through the war, but one that looks fairly new. I'm not suggesting you run out and buy an expensive attaché case. You can pick up a professional-looking case for around $50. The attaché case adds a touch of class, distinction, and professionalism. It never fails to impress interviewers. It doesn't matter whether you're carrying dirty laundry, a couple of hand grenades or a liter of whiskey. Your interviewer is not going to inspect its contents. Practically speaking, it's a great place to store a portfolio, your research, and a day planner.

Strategy 2: Know Your Industry and Your Work Background

It seems so obvious, you're probably wondering why I'm taking up space mentioning it. That's precisely why I did. Many job hunters look the part, but they don't go to the trouble to be on top of their industry. I've never understood why. The answer lies somewhere between laziness and naiveté. Take it from the pros and become a walking encyclopedia. Know where the action is, who the trendsetters are, who's in, out, and on the skids. *Critical:* Know everything you can about every company you're interviewing with. That includes its products, fast-trackers, significant achievements, sales, problems, and so on.

Along with knowing your industry front to back, know your work history like the back of your hand. Don't shrug your shoulders and say, "Of course I know my work background. I was there, wasn't I? How could I possibly forget?"

You'd be surprised how easily you forget dates, facts, and significant events, especially if you've had an active work life. If you've had four major jobs over the past decade, chances are you've forgotten many of the high points of each.

The letter you sent to this person captured his or her attention with important details of your career. During the interview you're expected to fill in the gaps and discuss jobs and experiences not included.

ADVICE

Make a list of the significant jobs you've held and the highlights of each one. All it takes is a little thought to pull up important events that can sell you. By the same token, you'll recall a string of details and screw-ups best forgotten. I guarantee this exercise will pay off. Won't you be pleasantly surprised when an interviewer asks, "Why don't you summarize your last two jobs?" Before the question is out of the interviewer's mouth, you're reeling off facts and figures, dazzling this person with your ability to remember the significant aspects of your work background.

Strategy 3: Get Ready to Field All Questions

Now to the meat of the interview. Let's find out what kinds of questions to expect. Whatever type of interview atmosphere is generated, all interviewers are waiting for you to deliver award-winning answers.

Memorizing answers to standard questions is not recommended. It seems stilted and rehearsed. A better idea is knowing what to expect so you can creatively pull up important details that apply to the job you want.

The smart job searcher is prepared for all types of interview questions. Although you may not know exactly what questions will be asked, you should know how to bat out the answers that will score home runs.

"What Is the Meaning of Life" to "What Were Your Responsibilities as Head Guillotine Designer?" Be Ready for General to Specific Questions

The questions you can expect will fall into two broad categories: general and specific. As you can guess, the hardest interviews are the ones in which they fling one general question after another. They're tougher for two reasons. First, they force you to think, and second, they require you to gather your thoughts and deliver answers that are terse and articulate. Specific questions, which we'll get to shortly, are straight-on questions with no interpretation required. You don't have to ask yourself, "What does he or she really mean? and "What is the best answer to it?"

Who, What, Where?

General questions fall into three broad categories: who, what, and where questions. Let's take a look at some general questions and find out how to tackle them. The most difficult general category is the "who" question. Take a deep breath, say a silent prayer, and brace yourself. There's an excellent chance you'll be asked moronic questions that have nothing to do with the job in question.

The underlying question is always

"Who are you?"

It has more to do with your personal attributes and motivations than with job-related skills. The trick is turning around the question and making it specific. No matter how bizarre, strangely worded, or indirect the question, the interviewer still wants to find out if you're qualified to handle the work. He or she is not interested in your views on child rearing, philosophy, sex, or the future of capitalism.

Let's say you're applying for a job as a regional sales manager of a large department store chain. It's a job that carries a good deal of responsibility and pays well. It's a buyer's market and the company is determined to find the best person for the job. As soon as you've made yourself comfortable, the interviewer flashes a broad smile and says,

"Tell me about yourself."

What do you say? A poor response is answering the question with a general answer such as, "I enjoy selling because I get to work closely with people and do a good bit of traveling. I'm the type of person who enjoys doing something new and challenging each day. And what could be more exciting than sales, where you're constantly meeting new people?"

Sorry, this applicant struck out. The above response told the interviewer practically nothing. Saying you enjoy working with people is not really explaining anything. If you're applying for a selling job, you're supposed to enjoy working with people. The real questions are: "Why do you enjoy working with people and what is it going to do for us?" and "What is it about selling that fires your imagination and adrenaline at the same time?"

Let's redo the scene, this time with a revealing positive, telling answer. "As far back as I can remember, I've enjoyed the challenge of convincing and selling others. There are three essential components of the selling equation. First, you have to believe in the product you're selling. Whether it's vacuum cleaners or computers, you have to believe they are the finest units on the market. Second, you must understand the product and be able to explain it. And last, you have to know how to convince others. Here lies the real challenge for the creative salesperson. That involves carefully and systematically explaining the product and how it can be beneficial to the user. Each job has been an important stepping-stone. As a regional sales manager, I will have the opportunity to further refine my selling strategies and to teach and supervise others. Clearly, there is more to selling than meets the eye."

A little wordy, but this applicant has the right idea. That's quite a difference from the first answer. The first answer is threadbare and inadequate, whereas the second is meaty and thoughtfully planned. The interviewer comes away with the impression that the applicant has given his job a great deal of thought and that he loves what he's doing. With those two assets working for him, it's not hard to conclude that he'd be perfect for the job.

Ready for some "what" questions? Now that you've got some practice with a "who are you" question, get ready for some more zingers from your interviewer. A popular, often-asked "what" question is

"What would you consider the perfect job?"

If you're not prepared, this could stump you too. If you can't deliver an answer that will please an interviewer, be creative and make it up. For example, I wouldn't tell interviewers that the perfect job is one that pays an extraordinary salary, has unbelievable benefits, and offers a short workday. The answer they'd like to hear is that the ideal job is the one for which you're applying. Of course, you can't use those exact words. But you can build a case for yourself by judiciously and diplomatically leading up to it. You could start with your last job, briefly touching on the reasons for moving (not because you hated your boss, had an ugly secretary, or found the food in the company cafeteria absolutely awful) and then lead into why you feel the job you're applying for is ideal.

Another tactic is simply to jump right in with an answer like: "The ideal job is one in which I can hone my talents, get maximum satisfaction, and thus help to make the company a leader in its industry. The ideal job is one that provides constant challenge and puts my abilities to the test. It's a stimulating environment that is mutually satisfactory for me and my employer. Using those criteria as a guide, I feel I can do some of my best work with your company."

The idea is to toot your own horn in a professional and straightforward manner. Don't beat around the bush. It's no crime to say you plan to climb the corporate ladder as fast as you can.

A few more "what" questions:

"What is important to you on a job?"

A variation on the earlier question. Again, get right to the heart of the issue. Don't open with money. You can mention it at the end, but initially do your utmost to convince the interviewer you're a company person, someone who is bright, enterprising, creative, and productive.

"What aspects of work do you enjoy most?"

The right answer applies directly to productivity and profits. You're being paid to do a job that will earn money for the company and help make the company stronger. Stress these aspects of work. Employers also love to hear answers relating to your creativity. The creative worker is a prized worker. He or she is the one who dares to try a new approach, test new concepts, and work on an idea through its various phases until it's realized. The creative worker constantly uses imagination and is excited by challenge. Stress these aspects of your personality and you're bound to make a favorable impression on your interviewer.

The flip side of the above question is

"What aspects of work do you enjoy least?"

Be careful. The interviewer is looking for an honest response, but don't make the mistake of getting too honest. You could wind up hanging yourself. If it's a highly technical or very creative job, you might play down one aspect of the job, such as paperwork. "I realize that the job carries a fair amount of unavoidable paperwork. While it's necessary, the real challenge is using my abilities and talent to solve creative problems." Whatever your real feelings are on this issue, try not to get too bogged down in negative details.

"What are your goals?"

Count on this one. Goal questions can be tricky if you don't know how to answer them. Be specific regarding long- and near-term goals. If you're applying for a job as an administrative assistant in a bank, don't tell the interviewer you want to be president one day. An answer like that will do more harm than good. Instead, show that you know something about working in a bank by listing the progression of jobs you hope to move through to become an assistant manager and finally a manager. These are realizable near- to intermediate-term goals. The interviewer will be impressed and think, "Here's a person with executive potential. There no telling how far she will go."

"What are your major strengths?"

Very similar to "What aspects of work do you enjoy most?" Major strengths should apply to nitty-gritty issues revolving around productivity and profits. If your major strengths can't benefit the company in a concrete way, what good are you and why should you be hired? Play up your strengths, staying just short of bringing in a New Orleans jazz band to accompany you while you tell the interviewer how great you are. Whether you're an architect, builder, programmer, urban specialist, or mason, you'll want to concentrate on strengths that demonstrate you do your job better than anyone else.

When discussing your strengths, it's a good idea to draw upon productive incidents from a prior job. "When I worked at Bundrally Architectural, a major solar project was almost abandoned because the company couldn't find a way to significantly cut its budget on materials. I gave it a good deal of thought and discovered that, instead of using an expensive hardwood, a special high-tension plexiglass could be used for practically half the cost."

By citing a specific incident, you cleverly show you have a head on your shoulders and are not reluctant to harness your creative juices to solve a tough problem.

Just when you've finished expanding upon your strengths, the interviewer may ask

"What is your greatest weakness?"

Again, try not to be too negative or too honest. Pull your punches by discussing something inconsequential. Mention that you have a tendency to lose track of time while involved in a major project and to concentrate on important problems, leaving superficial details to the last minute. It's a minor issue, but you're presenting it in such a way that it could almost be construed as an asset. You want the interviewer to think you're a nuts-and-bolts worker who'd rather sidestep the minor parts of the job to put all your energy into the important thought-provoking aspects of the job.

If you have to discuss a weakness—or anything negative, for that matter—make sure it's superficial and can be kept under control. Or present it in such a way that you give the impression your deficit is actually an asset.

Now a "where" question.

"Where do you see yourself 5 and 10 years down the road?"

The interviewer is simply asking a direct goal question. Ideal job candidates know where they are going, have their career mapped out in detail, and can tell you specifically where they hope to be 5 and 10 years from now. An obvious way of answering the question is to start by mentioning a long-term goal and then backtrack to the near- and intermediate-term goals that have to be conquered first. If you discuss your career in realistic terms, the interviewer quickly concludes that you're a hands-on practical person, as opposed to an idealistic and impractical dreamer.

To wind down, here are some other general questions you can expect.

"What made you choose this field?"

Almost guaranteed to be asked in every interview. Make sure you have an intelligent reason for choosing it. Don't answer "Because my dad is in it" or "There aren't too many fields in which you can earn more than $75,000 with only a couple of years of experience." Answers like these don't rack up points.

However you phrase your answer, make sure it includes the following points: (1) that you sincerely love the field, (2) that it provides untold satisfaction and challenges your imagination, and (3) that it allows creative growth. If there is some interesting history behind your choosing the field, mention it. If you have been fascinated with the field since you were a kid, elaborate on this fact. Many engineers, for instance, enjoy relating anecdotes that go back to their childhood. A mechanical engineer may spin a true story about how he built his own motorbike from scratch when he was in his midteens. Stories like this never fail to make an impression on an interviewer.

"Why did you leave your last job?"

Before you blurt out the ugly truth, think about your answer for a few moments. If you were fired for excessive lateness, for mismanaging an account, or for punching your supervisor in the nose, I'd think twice about confessing those truths to a prospective employer.

What should you say? If you want to get a job quickly, I'd find a happy medium between the truth and an outright lie. Whatever you decide, make sure it sounds believable and makes you look good. Even if you were fired because your company lost a major account, present the facts in such a way that the interviewer understands *you* had no control over the situation.

Put yourself in the employer's shoes. It stands to reason the employer would want to know all the details of why you left your last job. If the company went bankrupt, laid off half the staff, or closed the regional office you worked in because of sagging profits, all you have to do is present the facts. If the story is more complicated and involves, for example, a personality conflict between you and your supervisor that resulted in your getting the ax, a creative answer is necessary. A possible answer might go like this: "There was no room for growth. Over a 5-year period I advanced quickly, moving from training clerk to assistant supervisor overseeing the entire shipping department. At that point, I realized that my future with the company was limited. If I wished to advance, my best bet would be moving on to another company. Finally, I requested a raise but it was denied because the department was over budget. That's when I decided to find another job."

Obviously, the best negotiating position is to apply for a job while you're still employed. Not only do you have more leverage, but you have the time to make the best possible deal at your leisure. However, not everyone is so fortunate.

In conclusion, regardless of the conditions under which you left your last job, present a cogent story. And be careful with creative stories that are far from the truth. Chances are excellent that your prospective employer will call your former boss to find out what happened. Plan your strategy accordingly.

"What did you learn from your last job?"

Another popular one, since questions like these are excellent foundation builders leading into the reasons you applied for your most recent job. Employers want to see a strong element of consistency throughout your career. View each job as a stepping-stone or learning experience for something better. Let's say you're applying for a sales position and this is the second position of your career. "Working with an excellent supervisor, I learned a great deal about prospecting and account management and maintenance. In my second year with Rip-Off Bargains, I increased my account base 25 percent and worked on refining my telemarketing strategy. Now that I have a secure sales foundation, I feel confident and eager to take on more responsibility."

Whatever you say, make sure your prior job experience leads right to your respective employer's doorstep.

"Why do you want to work for us?"

A slight variation on this question is "What do you know about us?" The correct answer is not "Because you pay the highest salaries on the East Coast" or "Because you have the most liberal benefits package." These replies will not get you far. If you did your homework and researched the company, you know precisely where the company stands within its industry. You also know something about the company philosophy and its attitude toward the employees. Knowing all this, a cogent answer sounds something like: "Your company is well known as a leader in its industry. For the past half-decade, you've recorded an impressive growth record. Last year your new-product division's revenues outpaced those of your most aggressive competitor, Phat Rags, Ltd. What I find most exciting is that your R&D budget increases proportionately with your profits. Since this is the area I want to work in, your company represents a fabulous growth opportunity for me. You're a high-tech company that's ready to embrace the twenty-first century. With my background and credentials, I think it could be an ideal pairing for both of us."

With an answer like the above, it's hard not to be impressed. You've demonstrated that you know a good deal about the company and that you're sure of yourself.

If you happen to know something about the company's promotion policy, it might be beneficial to weave that into your answer. "I also like the idea that you prefer to hire from within your own ranks. This is marvelous, because it encourages your people to do their best."

Don't hesitate to reel off company statistics and industry projections, thus putting yourself in a good light.

"What do you do in your spare time?"

This sounds innocent enough, but beware. Companies want solid citizens who are involved in worthwhile pursuits on and off the job. If you're an incurable hedonist or an after-hours recluse, keep that information to yourself. But if you're a passionate sports enthusiast, part-time historian, writer, philosopher, animal rights activist, bird-watcher, or church organist, by all means mention it. Whatever your answer, demonstrate that you're an involved human being with an insatiable appetite for bettering yourself.

These are a few of the typical questions you can expect. Other questions will range from the direct to the indirect, from the expected to the bizarre. Be prepared to answer all of them. Remember that all questions—even the silly, seemingly inconsequential ones—are career-related. Tailor your answers accordingly.

Strategy 4: Grill the Interviewer

Once you field the 30- to 45-minute barrage of questions, it's your turn. If you didn't know it, let me be the first to inform you that an interview is a two-act melodrama. The first act is always the interviewer's, the second is all yours. Even if you did brilliantly in Act One and answered questions like a veteran actor in a Broadway play, you'll still get bad reviews if you fail to play in Act Two.

The best way to show sincere interest in a job is by asking questions about the company. This is when you get a chance to find answers to all the nitty-gritty questions that have been bothering you. It may not seem so, but you have more control over the outcome of your interview than you realize. Even though it's often a buyer's market, you have the power of choice. You've planned your moves like a professional chess player. Who's to say you won't get two or even three job offers? How will you know which is the best if you don't ask questions and find out?

Some of the questions below are obvious, others you probably didn't think you could ask.

"Is there much turnover in the position?"

This is where you plan on hanging out for a few years, at least. You may not be looking for a lifetime contract, but there is nothing wrong with wanting a little security. If you discover that your predecessor lasted only 3 months and there has been an unnerving amount of turnover over the past few years, I'd find out more information. After working this hard to land a job, you want to make sure you've picked the right one. You're entitled to know all the details.

"What are the reasons for the high turnover?"

The company may have good reasons for the turnover. There could have been interdepartmental problems which may have since been corrected. Or the interviewer may hedge and give you an incomplete answer, which necessitates learning more about the company before going any further.

"Has the job been recently created?"

In view of what's happening in the job market, this is a good question. New jobs are being created all over the place, presenting unique opportunities for highly motivated, aggressive workers. Newly created positions often offer greater opportunity for experimentation and creative expression.

By asking the above question, you may discover that the job has been around for many years, but major changes are on the horizon. The department may be on the verge of expanding or it may be merging with smaller departments, either of which points to exciting growth prospects.

"Have you been looking for someone for a long time?"

It's a great question which most interviewees are afraid to ask. Yet, you're entitled to know the answer. If the company has been looking for someone for 6 months, it can mean a couple of things. The company is very particular or it's not quite sure of who it wants. The answer to this question will help you structure your job campaign. If the job has been vacant for a long time, I'd pursue as many job leads as possible and not put all my eggs in one basket. You may be just what they're looking for and be presented with an offer almost instantly, or they could keep you on the edge of your seat for months until they make a decision. If you need a job immediately, you can't take any chances waiting around for a job that may never materialize.

"What type of person are you looking for?"

The interviewer asked you probing questions about your strengths, weaknesses, feelings about work, and why you think you're the ideal person for the job. There is no reason you can find out exactly what the company is looking for from the horse's mouth. Don't be surprised if the interviewer smiles at your candid inquisitiveness. You may be surprised when the interviewer pulls out an elaborate job specification sheet and discusses some of the job characteristics and qualifications. No matter how you look at it, you're bound to learn something and come out ahead by asking this question.

"How many employees staff the department and to whom will I report?"

Solid question. You should know whom you'll be working with. The smart job applicant goes into a new job knowing as much about the position as possible. By knowing the reporting structure, you'll know something about the internal working of the company. Is it an unwieldy bureaucracy or a streamlined company with clear sight lines to the executive suite?

"What kind of promotional opportunities does the job provide?"

Critical issue. If you're a hot property, the company's promotional machinery can elevate you to a position of wealth and power. But if the company lacks clearly defined promotional procedures, be wary. Many employee-centered companies review workers for salary increases and promotions every 6 months. This means you could have the opportunity to bolt through the ranks at a rapid-fire clip—if you're motivated.

"Do you provide in-house training or are employees responsible for keeping up with developments in their field?"

If you're in a high-tech field, this is an important issue. It means constant education and retraining throughout your career. The majority of companies involved in high-technology projects provide in-house training for their workers. The reasons are not altruistic either. Yes, employees benefit, but staying ahead of the pack is also smart business.

If you're management-bound, many medium and large companies send capable workers back to college for advanced degrees. Considering the cost of college these days, it's worth hanging onto a job you're not crazy about just to get an advanced degree.

"Will I be required to travel?"

Many companies hedge on this issue, especially when a good deal of travel is required. When a company says 15 percent of your time will be spent traveling, find out what that means. The company could be lowballing a true figure of 25 percent, which amounts to a good deal of time away. If you have little tots, you may not want to be away from home that much. But if you're single, the prospect of spending a lot of time on the road may be an exciting inducement. If it's a sales job, expect to do a fair share of traveling.

Other important issues often glossed over in interviews concern retirement/pension and medical packages. The higher you go on the corporate ladder, the more benefits you're likely to get. Many companies give you a choice of medical plans and retirement plans.

Similarly, find out what kind of vacation allowance you'll be offered. Many companies also have vacation bonus programs. If you perform exceptionally, you may find yourself sitting in the lap of luxury on some Caribbean or Hawaiian island on behalf of the company. Not bad. If that isn't an incentive to work hard, I don't know what is.

Finally,

"When do you expect to make a decision?"

Don't leave until you have some idea when you're going to hear from the company again. This is valuable information for planning your job campaign. If you learn, for instance, that the company just started interviewing for the position, it's safe to assume a decision won't be made for at least 3 weeks, if not longer. But, if you were the next-to-last applicant interviewed, a decision should not be far off. It pays to know where you stand. If it looks like there will be a long waiting period until the company makes a decision, move on. Instead, I'd aggressively expend my energy in several directions at once. There is nothing wrong with the scatter-gun approach if you go about it right.

Let's wrap it up by summarizing some of the important points in turning out a slam-bang performance.

Interview Fast Facts
Rehearse! Rehearse! Rehearse!

We've covered the types of interviews, appropriate dressing for the meeting, and potential questions. Now let's wind down with a potpourri of facts, tips, and reminders.

Uppermost, rehearse interview scenarios. Think about potential questions and speak your answers out loud so you can hear how they sound. Regarding your interview interaction skills, mind the following:

- *Handshake.* Don't make a big deal about the handshake. A quick, firm, and confident handshake is recommended. No Superman bone-crushing tactics to prove you can leap tall buildings in a single bound. At the other extreme, no wimpy, limp handshakes either. The interviewer may think you're unsure of yourself.
- *Posture.* Don't try to look like a marine. Find a comfortable posture with your back straight and shoulders square. Avoid slouching in your chair.
- *Voice level.* No shouting, mumbling, or whispering. Just speak at a comfortable level that can be heard. If you've practiced answering questions with a tape recorder, you should have a clear idea of how you sound.
- *Eye contact.* Don't stare. There is a big difference between making eye contact and staring down the person. The goal is having comfortable and relaxed eye contact.

No-no questions. What do you do if asked an off-putting, personal, inappropriate, or illegal question? There are no pat answers. According to the Equal Employment Opportunity Commission (EEOC), interviewers are not permitted to ask questions about race, religion, age, sex, or political affiliation. Yet, if an employer crosses the line, what can you say that doesn't jinx your chances of being considered for the job? "Hey, look Mr. Bozobrain, you just violated EEOC rules and asked me an illegal question. If you don't want me to take legal action, I'd rephrase that if I were you." With a response like that, what do you think your chances are of being considered? You'd be correct if you said horrific. So pick your battles carefully. If asked an inappropriate question, straighten out the interviewer without verbally bullwhipping him or her. If you want the job, diplomatically avoid the issue and be cool. Often, employers don't mean to be offensive and have no idea they asked an illegal question. Whoever said bosses have a monopoly on brains and tact?

Finally, one last bit of precious advice: *Be yourself.* Don't try to sound like the perfect interviewee. Just express yourself in your own unique way. A high-powered Chicago headhunter said the perfect job applicant is someone who is comfortable in his or her own skin. Heed that precious advice.

CHAPTER 18

SO WHADDAYA GONNA PAY ME?

RULE 18 **Don't be uptight about tactfully negotiating a great deal for yourself.**

Congratulations! Your award-winning interview performance landed you a job offer. But wait to hoist a few to celebrate, because the game ain't over yet. It's great to know you've captured a job; the next big hurdle is getting a decent salary.

Here's where job seekers universally screw up. They're so delighted to land a job, they just sit back and take any salary dished out. The reasoning goes something like this: "I'd better shut my mouth and take what they offer or they'll find someone else."

That's absolutely crazy thinking, elevating paranoia to an intergalactic dimension.

What's the Big Deal? It's Only Money!

Let's analyze the situation. You're in a fantastic position. Ninety-five percent of the tension has been lifted from your shoulders. Unless the salary is exactly what you wanted—which seldom happens—you must tactfully up the ante to approach your money mark. To do so, you must negotiate. And that causes problems for most people. A great many of us have difficulty with the wonderful green stuff. We love it but think we ought to loathe it. The irony is we spend 50 to 60 hours a week working for money, yet we won't sit down and try to make the best money deal possible. A prominent Los Angeles shrink said most people would rather talk about their sex lives than about how much they earn and what money means to them.

So don't beat yourself up if you have a money hang-up. Instead, painlessly defuse the money issue by asking yourself the following two questions.

1. *What would a great salary mean to you?* This ought to be a no-brainer. The little wheels in your head should be whirling at warp speed. That's right, it would mean no money woes, buy what you want when you want it, take fabulous vacations, and live worry-free. So I've exaggerated, but you get the idea.
2. *What would happen if you tactfully negotiated the best salary deal you could?* Remember, this is the mid-1990s not the early 1930s. The work place has changed radically. For the most part, deplorable working conditions are gone forever. Most employers are treating their workers equitably and providing a platform for growth. A competitive market has taught them that feisty, ambitious workers who are unafraid to speak up for themselves are a prized commodity. Practically speaking, after investing time and money in the process, employers want to wrap up the deal quickly and get back to work. Interviewing applicants amounts to a huge headache they don't want to repeat.

Playing the Salary Game

Still squeamish about negotiating? Consider this powerful reason: By intelligently and maturely negotiating salary, you present yourself as a polished professional. As soon as you speak up for yourself, you're considered an individualist, someone who will fight for himself or herself. You're not a rank-and-file person but someone with the potential to climb the organization ladder. That's right, you exhibit superstar potential. In short, you appear as someone who's not intimidated and is ready and willing to play the salary game. Confident job hunters see salary negotiation as an enormous game.

Career writer Marilyn Moats Kennedy talks about the myth surrounding salary negotiating in her book *Salary Strategies.* Kennedy says job searchers are under the impression that some gigantic mysterious, all-knowing corporate force determines salary levels for workers. She refers to this bureaucratic force as the mysterious "they."

The revelation that there is no omnipotent "they" should allay fears and blow this myth to smithereens. Don't believe employers when they say the salary is "firm" or "the final offer." If they want you, they'll negotiate.

Put it all together and you have more bargaining power than you realize. Don't let it slip through your fingers. Take the hint and don't accept just any salary dropped in your lap.

Tactful and Diplomatic Applicants Cop the Big Rewards
Don't Ever Blow Your Cool

Knowing you can negotiate and knowing how to do it are two different stories. No matter how tough it is, the smart negotiator is prepared for a long siege. If you're lucky, the entire process will be wrapped up in an hour. The negotiations will go something like this:

"We're prepared to offer you $65,000, Ms. Braun, plus a complete medical and retirement package."

"That's a very generous offer, Mr. Gehrung, but that's only slightly more than I was earning at Bombs 'R' Us, Inc. Based upon my experience and understanding of the armaments industry, $73,500 is a more equitable salary."

"I understand where you're coming from, Ms. Braun. I would like our relationship to start off on the right foot. Let's shake hands on a salary of $73,500 and talk about our benefits package."

Many negotiations actually proceed that effortlessly. Most, however, require more discussion. Plenty also drag out over several days. Holding it all together when an employer wants to get you as cheaply as possible requires mental, even physical, stamina. After all, you're only human. When this back-and-forth discussion is going on, you're thinking to yourself, "This guy runs a $300 million company and he's reluctant to pay me $8000 more than I was making on my last job. I don't know how much more of this I can take. If it keeps up, I may lose my temper and hurl the little cheapskate out of his twentieth-story window."

A perfectly normal feeling. Nevertheless, the idea is to never let an employer pick up even a trace of impatience, anger, or frustration on your part. No matter how long it takes, hang in there. Employers who are reluctant to agree to salary terms may try commonly used stall tactics to get you to agree to their terms. "Why don't you give me a couple of days to ponder our offer, Mr. Machiavelli?" Or, "Since you're asking for more than we planned to spend, I'd like to discuss your request with my partners. They're going to have to agree to it."

Even though the above employers are talking out of both sides of their mouths, their tactics succeed in generating anxiety. They're putting you on hold and dangling you like a puppet on a string. The worst part is they didn't tell you when they would get back to you. Naturally, paranoia gets the best of you and you become convinced that you've blown it. ("They hate me. I should have taken the offered salary and been done with it. I know they're going to hire someone else now.") It's okay to think these thoughts, but whatever you do, *don't* act on them. Take a deep breath, sit back and wait, and tell yourself the following: "I haven't blown it. They're just making me sweat. I know we'll arrive at a happy middle ground."

And they will work with you for a very obvious reason: *They don't want to lose you.* What you want to avoid is underselling yourself by agreeing to a salary that's less than you feel you deserve. You'll abort all your hard work and make a bad impression. Waiting is hell, but hang tough. The employer will either meet or come close to meeting your terms.

ADVICE

Be prepared to handle high-pressure tactics. Keep up your guard. Some bosses can be deceptively subtle. The idea is to never appear needy. Even though you're wearing the only suit you own and you owe 5 months of back rent, make the employer think your financial situation couldn't be sturdier.

To get you in shape for salary negotiations, study these five commandments.

Five Salary-Negotiating Commandments

Commandment 1: Know What You're Worth
How Salaries Are Determined

It's shocking to think that many applicants don't have a clue what they're worth in the job market. Once again, remember what you are to employers. You're a product, overhead, an expense on the balance sheet. All they care about is whether that expense is justified.

Salaries are determined by examining three important factors:

1. Salaries on prior jobs
2. Individual strengths
3. Industry salary ranges

The first two are obvious, the sources for the third are as follows.

- *Want ads.* Newspaper want ads give you a snapshot of salaries in your industry. Follow them religiously and you'll get a panoramic picture of what large, medium-size, and small companies are paying.

- *Trade associations and professional groups.* The larger the trade organization, the more statistics it publishes, and the more reliable the information. The well-financed ones, such as associations in the paper, oil, food, tobacco, entertainment, and music industries, publish annual salary surveys of companies throughout the United States. This is valuable information, especially if you're considering relocating. An electrical or chemical engineer with 3 to 5 years of experience, for example, will probably earn more money in a large city like New York or Los Angeles than in Mansfield, OH, or Boise, ID.
- *U.S. Department of Labor's Bureau of Labor Statistics.* Most job searchers don't realize that our government is a wealth of information. The bureau publishes special reports and the yearly *Occupational Outlook Handbook*. It's excellent for providing concrete information about job and industry forecasts, yet is unreliable when it comes to current salary information. Salary information is at least a year old. In high-demand fields like computer design, salaries can change dramatically from year to year. Don't follow government salary ranges as gospel. For updated information, call your state labor department. It may have more current figures.
- *Headhunters.* Call executive recruiters or headhunters specializing in your field. If you're lucky and reach a friendly staffer, he or she may tell you what salary levels are like and may even pass on some negotiating tips. Since recruiters talk to companies daily, the information couldn't be more current.

Commandment 2: Connect with the Company Understand Its Goals and Vision

You demonstrated enough interest in the company for the employer to make you a job offer. Now it's time to show you have an even greater understanding of the company's inner workings. Now is the time for persuasive selling. You can justify more money by highlighting your impressive background. "With my 10 years in product development, I feel I'm justified in asking for the higher end of the salary range. Having created and managed targeted promotional campaigns, I know I can launch your company's new no-fat, no-calorie, no-cholesterol chocolate mousse."

While building a strong case for yourself, cite facts and figures when possible. By the time you stop talking, the employer may think, "Wow, this woman is impressive. She knows stuff about the company that our own people don't even know."

Commandment 3: Drive Home Accomplishments

At the same time you're impressing the employer with your knowledge of the company, constantly stress your accomplishments. "I've spent 15 years honing my programming skills, Mr. Mussolini. I've made it a point to stay on top of all the new technologies. I'm well versed in all computer languages and can apply them comfortably. With your current needs, this is an important asset. I don't have to be trained. I can be productive from day one. This is why I feel I'm entitled to an additional $50 a week. I'm not asking for anything I didn't earn." Excellent! This applicant is pushing all the right buttons. She's not just saying she is an incredible programmer, she's proving it. That's what good negotiating is all about. You score points by making powerful bottom-line points. Employers love to hear that you can hit the ground running. That spells profits, and profits are what business is all about.

Commandment 4: Argue Logically

Not everyone thinks, speaks, or writes logically. In fact, some people are so illogical, one wonders how they wound up in powerful jobs. Maybe it's because they have no clue what they're doing, yet somehow managed to convince everyone they're brilliant by not making any sense. Be prepared for illogical and irrational negotiators who try to bluff you with doublespeak and gobbledygook. Stay centered and argue logically and methodically. If you pick up the employer's beat, you're sure to get nowhere fast. But stick to the issues and the conversation will swing back to the topic at hand: your salary demands.

A common diversionary tactic is for employers to go off on a tangent and glorify the company as a means of enticing you into taking the offer. The employer might say something like, "You know we hire the cream of the crop, Mr. Bundy. We get over 12 million applications a year plus 15 million résumés, yet we hire only seven programmers annually. You belong to an elite group. Maybe you aren't aware of it, but we are the premier hand grenade manufacturer in the country. There are more than 300 companies in this tiny industry, yet we have the distinction of being the oldest, largest, and best. This is a well-documented fact throughout the industry."

With flag-raising statements like these, the employer is hoping you'll say: "I see what you mean. I never thought of it. I don't know why I'm making such a big deal about an additional $100 a week. This *is* the best company in the industry and I'm honored to join the team. I'll take the salary you offered. When can I start work?"

If you say anything that remotely sounds like the above rah-rah speech, I'll never let you read another one of my books. Whatever happens, stick to your position.

Commandant 5: Know When to Compromise

Most times, negotiations will get you a salary close to your mark. But sometimes the employer can't budge from the stated salary. And there are good reasons for this. What do you do?

1. Punch the employer in the nose and call him a big, fat jerk.
2. Throw yourself on the floor and have a screaming temper tantrum like you did when you were 5 years old.
3. Compromise.

If you picked 3, you are correct. Mature, career-minded adults work toward a compromise. You've come this far. Why blow it all and go back to square one and start pounding the pavement again? You've gotten this far because you and the company are in sync. It looks like a good marriage. Go to the next step and try to make it work. For a little while, at least.

Companies often can't meet all salary demands for reasons that run from budget cutbacks, a recent downswing, or expansion to depressed sales.

The big question is: How do you compromise? Consider these options:

- Take less, but ask for a 6-month performance review, rather than the traditional annual review, so you can be bumped up to the salary you originally requested. Once you've proven yourself, the company will feel a lot better about meeting your demands.
- Agree to a lower salary until a sales or productivity goal is met. At that point, your salary will be increased.
- Consider a contract or consulting arrangement. If it doesn't look like the company will meet your demands for a long time, try working for the company on a contract basis. Because you're an independent contractor and not an employee, you stand to make more money because the company doesn't take any taxes out of your pay. However, you will have to pay your own taxes.

ADVICE

Be flexible and open to alternative working arrangements. You never know where they'll lead.

Try a contract arrangement for 6 months and you'll know how to proceed. At a time when companies are aggressively pursuing contingent working relationships, it's a great way to get to know the company and vice versa. Who's to say you won't prefer this kind of working relationship? Or, after a short period of time, the company may come back to you with your original offer or better. You really can't lose.

Let's move on by solidifying the deal in writing.

CHAPTER 19

WRAP UP THE DEAL

RULE 19 Put the employment agreement in writing so the working arrangement can be mutually agreed upon by employer and worker.

Now, we're in the home stretch. Take a deep breath. The worst is over, the rest is easy. Before you get all revved up to start your new job, there is one last bit of important business that has to be concluded. It's a detail most job hunters never consider. Put the agreement in writing. It's a professional touch that sidesteps embarrassing moments later on.

Why a Letter?

It's very easy for misunderstandings to occur. In your excitement to capture the job, important issues may have been glossed over. Or the employer might have explained something that went in one ear and out the other. You don't want to be in the awkward position of righting the company later on. A letter serves the following purposes:

1. *It details the working relationship.* A letter precisely explains responsibilities, salary, and so on.
2. *It provides an opportunity to put your expectations on paper.* If there are discrepancies about your responsibilities, the time to

correct them is before you start your job. The amount of travel, for example, is a common bone of contention for many workers. Employers have a knack for underestimating the amount of travel required. A prospective employer may say the job requires 15 percent travel, yet 2 months into the job you find you're spending at least 2 days every week on the road. While it may be impossible to accurately describe all your job functions and responsibilities, the letter gives you a chance to come close.

REMEMBER: A five- or six-line job description can't fully describe a job.

3. *It describes how you can be terminated.* It sounds gruesome, but termination is an issue that ought to be dealt with in your letter. Remember, this is the end of the 1990s and job security is practically an oxymoron. There are no safety nets. Judging by what's been happening over the past decade, odds are you won't be working in the same place 4 years from now. What happens if you're fired—sorry, terminated? You don't want your employer to call you in at 10 a.m. and ask you to clear your desk so you can be permanently gone by 5 p.m. Yet it happens every day. Whatever the circumstances of your being axed, you want to be treated equitably and be given at least 2, maybe 3, weeks' notice.
4. *It strengthens your bargaining position.* If there is a takeover, consolidation, or merger, you can present the letter to your new employer. It doesn't mean you'll keep your job, but it could score you some points. Your new boss might think, "This guy had sense enough to put his employment agreement in writing. It shows he's a professional, the kind of person who puts everything on the table and is not afraid to speak up."

It Is Not a Legal Document

Keep in mind the letter will not hold up in court if you sue your employer for misrepresenting a job, or have discrepancies over pay, working hours, or benefits. However, if there ever is a legal hassle, the letter would certainly bolster your case by giving credence to your allegations. It wouldn't be a bad idea to file a copy of your letter with your attorney, just in case.

But this is really a secondary purpose of the letter. The primary reason is to clarify the job before you begin work.

The Letter's Contents

The letter ought to answer the following questions:

1. What are my responsibilities?
2. Where will I be working? A private office? Cubicle? Open space module? The subbasement next to the heating system?
3. Whom will I be working with?
4. Whom will I report to?
5. What are my hours?
6. What is the salary, commission structure, incentive pay, and so on?
7. How much travel will be required?
8. What are the benefits (medical and life insurance, vacations) and perks (car, expense account)?
9. What are my promotion opportunities? When will I be reviewed?

Sample Letter

Let's put together a sample letter. Keep the letter short and sweet. Ideally, it should be less than a page. Consider this sample format.

June 23, 19XX

Ms. Eva Last
Pretty Things, Inc.
24 Armanstrasse Boulevard
Trinity, PA XXXXX

Dear Ms. Last:

This letter summarizes the employment agreement between Sergio Bonaparte and Pretty Things, Inc. On Monday, I am scheduled to begin work as sales manager of the southwest region of the United States. Two assistant managers, who track and evaluate accounts on a weekly basis, will report to me. My direct supervisor is Otto Frederick Menguile, an assistant vice president reporting directly to the president. Once my budgets and field strategies are approved by Mr. Menguile, my job is to implement them and make sure they work. To get the necessary input from the field, I'll be expected to devote 10 to 15 percent of my time to travel. Typically, I can expect to spend more time on the road during the heavy Christmas and Easter selling seasons.

My salary will be $85,000 a year, plus a 15 percent commission on new accounts. I am to be reviewed after my first 6 months, rather than waiting for the traditional yearly review. If I boost sales in my region by at least 15 percent, my salary will be increased by a minimum of 15 percent.

A company car will also be at my disposal while employed at Pretty Things.

I'm entitled to 3 weeks' paid vacation a year. After 3 years with the company, I will be given 4 weeks' paid vacation annually. I'll also get a company-paid medical plan, covering hospitalization and doctor's visits for me and my family. After 5 years with the company, I will be entitled to a pension plan.

If terminated for not meeting job goals or for other job-related reasons, I will be given 3 weeks' notice plus 3 weeks' pay for every year I worked at the company.

Sincerely,

Sergio Bonaparte (Date)
Eva Last (Date)

Don't expect your prospective boss to sign off on the letter. Chances are you'll have to make some changes. Your boss may not buy your severance arrangement. It would be great if he or she gave you 3 weeks' pay for every year worked, but don't bet on it. Remember, severance pay is an ethical responsibility, not a legal requirement. Even if you're the best worker the company has ever had, an employer is not required to give you severance pay, or for that matter, 2 to 3 weeks' notice either. While chances are likely it won't happen, you can be axed after completing your first day on the job.

Once the letter is signed and dated, give a copy to your boss and keep the original. As suggested, mail a copy to your attorney just in case there are ever legal problems.

The smart job hunter takes no chances. Whether you stay for a decade or take a better job in 2 years, you'll most likely never see the employment letter again. *But* you never know.

Now let's make the most of the job experience and talk about some practical on-the-job tips.

CHAPTER 20

LEARN TO BE A GOOD SERVANT

RULE 20 Smart employees turn themselves into skilled followers.

What? Become a follower? What kind of talk is that? I'm me. I'm my own man (or woman). I'm not a mindless servant and I won't kiss anyone's feet. Heck, this is the liberated 1990s, the decade of employees' rights, affirmative action, and all that stuff. I don't intend to take any guff from anyone—not even my boss.

If you actually believe this, then you'll believe I'm going to be the next president of the United States. Don't go overboard with all that flag-raising, idealistic garble. You may be an heir to the DuPont estate and one of the smartest people on the planet, but as soon as you take a job, you join the ranks of paid followers. You're an employee reporting to a boss. Don't lose sight of that reality.

You'll luck out if your boss appreciates you from the onset, but don't bet on it. More likely, you'll have to work on making that happen. Count on personality, temperament, and work style differences. But your goal from day one should be to build a harmonious working relationship with your boss so you both can do your best work.

STRATEGY: The only way to hold on to your job and ascend the corporate ladder is by transforming yourself into a smart follower. It doesn't mean selling your soul to the devil either. It means playing the company game like a pro. Management consultant Ira Chaleff makes the same point in his book *The Courageous Follower: Standing up to and for Our Leaders* (Berrett-Koehler).

Who Said You Have to Be a Leader?

In a country that extols rugged individualism, followers have taken a bad rep. Dozens of books advise on how to be a leader, but how many books have you seen about being a follower? Give Chaleff points for being a feisty contrarian. He says that both numerically and temperamentally, there are far more followers than leaders. There is very little guidance, however, on how to follow in such a way that both you and the organization profit.

Ironically, Chaleff points out that while we make a big fuss about becoming leaders, from birth we're trained to be passive followers. Says Chaleff:

> Our early conditioning about leadership takes place in childhood, at home, and at school, where others are held responsible for our behavior but we are not held responsible for theirs. The power of our early conditioning is so strong that for most of us, it is an act of courage to confront a leader about counterproductive behavior, instead of an ordinary act of relationship.

Put it all together and you're left with an inescapable conclusion: According to the divine order of the universe, followers will always outnumber leaders. And since we're practically bred to be followers, it pays to understand the follower's role.

Welcome to the Real World
Smart Followers Finish First

In this frenetic corporate climate of unrelenting downsizings, there are redeeming benefits to being a good follower. Beyond positioning yourself for higher-paying jobs, you're buying time in a volatile work place. Smart followers position themselves so cleverly that they're hardly seen or heard. They don't stand out from the crowd, yet their presence is felt. They've mastered the game by knowing how to write the book on correct corporate behavior. They know when to be silent and when to put in their 2 cents.

Great followers are political experts when it comes to making the organization work for them. They're not finks, stool pigeons, or goody-good butt kissers. Instinctively, they know their place and never step out of character. A carefully honed survival instinct keeps them focused.

Who's Got the Power?

Not everyone can thrive in an organization. The ones who make it are social animals who have mastered the art of human interaction. The best can get along with anyone—from tyrants to weak-kneed bosses afraid of their own shadows. They understand the power structure, respect the corporate chain of command, and have no problem taking orders.

Uppermost, good followers know how the real world works and they don't attempt to change it. There's something to be said for accepting things the way they are. It certainly makes things easier. Intuitively, they know that as soon as you have a group of three or more people, a leader emerges. The group is content to follow the leader's command with no qualms about the relationship.

It takes astute followers about a week on the job to psych out the organization. By then, they've tapped into the grapevine and know who the power players are. They know the superstars, who's hanging in limbo, and who's on the way out. It adds up to critical information that helps them build their special niche.

Three Rules for Smart Following

1. *Become indispensable.* Here's where basic psychology pays off. Observe your boss so you can find out how he or she thinks. The goal is to be indispensable. It's easy when you agree with your

boss and identify with his or her mission and fight the same battles. However, when you're at ideological odds, it's tougher. Then, personal decisions are necessary.

Explore your goals and values. You've hit the bull's-eye if they are pretty much the same as your boss's. But if there are personal, material, ethical, or moral differences, you've got to make a decision. Can you overcome these differences so they don't get in the way of building a strong relationship? These are issues only you can sort out.

2. *Make your boss look good.* Respecting the logic of the power structure, smart followers go out of their way to make their boss stand out. They make sure their boss knows it too. Smart followers are not martyrs; they're pragmatists looking out for number one. The better the boss looks, the better they look. Once your boss appreciates your value, you're reasonably secure. If he or she moves up the ladder, you're almost certain to move too.

   Also, be ready to defend your boss against hostile attacks from inside or outside company ranks. This also makes you look great. Count on the grapevine for making your boss aware of your unwavering loyalty. Every time you stand up for the boss, you leap the trust ladder a few rungs at a time. If you get the chance to rescue your boss from pending disaster, bail the boss out of a tight situation, or correct a glaring mistake, you've come as close to achieving sainthood as any employee can. At that point, you've graduated to artful follower.

3. *Be visible.* Smart followers don't crawl into a corner and collect their paychecks. They do just the opposite and work at being visible. They volunteer for projects and take on as much responsibility as possible so they make themselves, their boss, and the organization look good.

   When necessary, they'll work late to help meet a tight deadline. Or they'll cover for the boss by coming in on Saturday so he or she can get away for a weekend. A little calculated self-sacrifice goes a long way. Toss all these attributes into the pot and you've got a powerful stew that never fails to win accolades for you.

CHAPTER TWENTY

No One Says You Have to Be a Lackey or Scapegoat Either!

Smart followers are not fools. The best have a finely tuned sense of self-worth. They know who they are, what they want, where they're going, and, uppermost, how to get there. They also know how far they can be pushed and what their limits are. Smart bosses know this about their troops.

Chaleff distinguishes between just following and being a courageous follower. Blind followers will follow their boss over a cliff if necessary. They're great in a war, but dangerous in a corporation. They do whatever they are told, never editing their commands. That's okay if you lack a moral and ethical gyroscope with no sense of right from wrong. Most of us, however, are not built that way. Courageous followers, on the other hand, are principled. Naturally, there'll be plenty of times they'll have to take a deep breath, shut their mouths, and keep their opinions to themselves. But they'll sleep nights knowing these were minor issues. Yet there'll be other occasions when they can't abide by what Chaleff calls the old-fashioned "I know nothing" style of followership. That's repugnant. If there is blatant wrongdoing, courageous followers won't allow themselves to look the other way.

It sounds noble, but the downside is that courageous followers often get in trouble by opening their mouths once too often. Some become whistle-blowers, calling their leaders on destructive behavior and also alienating themselves from their peers. It's a utopian situation when you can disagree with your boss on big issues and still keep your job. Don't count on that happening.

Remember: You often pay a price for being a courageous follower.

Thankfully, most of us are not faced with these decisions. Most relationships with superiors fall within tame, controllable, and nonthreatening boundaries. We seldom face situations calling for potentially job-threatening decisions.

Finally, courageous followers are not "yes" men and women, according to Chaleff. They don't orbit around their leader. The trick is asserting your ideas while respecting and diplomatically bowing to your leader's opinions. It sounds good on paper, but if you and your boss have forceful personalities, backing off takes more fortitude than you realize.

The command word for becoming a smart follower is *harmony.* First, achieve harmony with yourself by being clear about your goals; second, achieve harmony with your boss to develop a smooth, even fun, working relationship. If you have all that in order, you've become a perfect follower, securing your position until there is a change of command.

Let's move on and find out how to pack our bags—just in case.

CHAPTER 21

MAKE SURE YOUR BAGS ARE ALWAYS PACKED

Don't get too comfortable. Always have one foot out the door.

If you expect to pounce on opportunities as soon as they present themselves, you'd better be a "Traveling Man" (or woman), to quote the title of Ricky Nelson's classic hit. Figuratively speaking, it means being ready to move down that lonesome career highway at a moment's notice. The survivalist's mindset will keep you sharp, the master of your own fate, and, most important, steadily employed. Like a sprinter at the starting line waiting for the start of the race, you'll always be ready.

No matter how enticing the job seems, don't think you've found a home and perfect job all in one neat package. If you think that way, you've fallen into the same fantasy moat that trapped our parents and grandparents. Instead, think of every job as a rest stop along the career highway. How long you'll hold a job is anyone's guess. You wouldn't be wrong thinking it's only temporary.

Four Survival Strategies for Staying Employed

1. *Don't get too comfortable.* I'm not suggesting you be a doom-and-gloomer, just a hardheaded pragmatist. Don't be seduced by enticing promises like "You're doing a heck of a job, Lucretia. Hiring you was the smartest thing we ever did. In a couple of years, budget permitting, I'm going to try to bump you up to manager."

Hearing that type of praise is enough to make anyone think she's found the perfect job. It's only normal to occasionally think you've found a career home and to fantasize about spending the next 20 years with the company. But make sure this is only a passing thought, which is replaced by coldhearted pragmatism. Yes, it could happen. But I wouldn't run out and put a down payment on an expensive car.

REMEMBER: Job security is a myth.

Think like a fatalist. Yes, you can control your working environment to a certain degree by doing a great job and building strong relationships. Otherwise, you're at the whim of the winds of change. You don't know what's coming around the corner. A closed-door decision could put you back on the street so fast your head will spin. Most always, you'll have no control over it. It could be that a merger or restructuring is taking place, and the last one hired (that's you) is the first to go. No, it's not cruel and heartless. It's just a fact of life. One day, a human resources person will summon you and tell you, "There was a redeployment of resources. We're sorry to tell you, Eddie, but you've been decruited. That means you were deselected, dehired. In plain English, Eddie, you've been canned, fired. Don't forget to turn over your office key when you leave today. Good luck."

2. *Track your accomplishments.* For the above reason, you must meticulously track your accomplishments so you're ready to peddle your wares elsewhere. Try to do it systematically by keeping a log or diary so entries are made weekly. Every time you have a victory—hit a sales quota, create a winning advertising campaign, or conquer a promotion—make note of it.

REMEMBER: It's easy to lose track of important accomplishments. Don't be negligent about this critical task.

3. *Build your network.* The best time to beef up your network is while you're employed. It's great to be able to take home a weekly

paycheck, but don't get lazy just because you're comfortably paying your bills. Lunch and afterwork hours and slow periods ought be devoted to building contacts and career-long relationships.

4. *Save your money.* No matter how disciplined you think you are, it's easy to spend more than you have to when you have a paycheck rolling in every week. You say to yourself, "I'll start socking away a healthy percentage of my paycheck 6 months from now. I'm safe until then. Meanwhile, I want to enjoy life and not stint."

   It's not that you don't deserve to indulge yourself, yet I urge you resist these temptations. You don't have to keep eating pasta and tuna fish, but it does mean you ought to monitor your spending and sock away as much as possible.

ADVICE

Rather than stick 10 to 15 percent of your paycheck in a savings account, create a separate emergency fund. This is a special account that will be used if you're laid off. Yes, there's an excellent chance you could be laid off again. So don't deceive yourself about this reality. The emergency fund serves a dual purpose: both practical and psychological. Not only are you socking money away in case you're laid off, but I guarantee you'll sleep better knowing you're thinking like a clear-headed pragmatist. You're not waiting for anybody to take care of you. You're doing it yourself. That's something to celebrate.

If you're still around in 6 months, I urge you to do a job tune-up, which we'll get to in the next chapter.

CHAPTER 22

UH OH, IT'S TIME FOR A JOB TUNE-UP

Every 6 months, find out whether you still love your job.

Let's jump ahead to the future. Six months have bolted by and you're still at the same company. The way things are going, it looks like you're going to be there for another year. Terrific!

Just because you've settled into a comfortable situation and feel reasonably secure, that's no reason to abandon thoughts of moving on and considering other jobs.

ADVICE

Don't get lazy. Don't stick with a job just because it's comfortable and there is a promise of security. Stay for the right reasons—namely, you love the work, the people, and the money. You should feel motivated, challenged, and content.

This is why you ought to do a job tune-up every 6 months—to find out answers to the following questions.

1. *Do you still love your job?* It's no crime if you don't. It's easy to be seduced by embellished job descriptions which are embossed by human resources people or employers who don't have a clue about what the job entails. It happens all the time. Six months into the job, you find it's really a job for three people or, it's so hopelessly boring, you can do it blindfolded in 4 hours and coast the remaining 4.
2. *What do you love about the job?* You shouldn't have to think about it. If you love your job, you might say, "Most every morning I'm eager to get to work. Every day is different, bringing new challenges and projects. The days fly by. Often, it's 3 p.m. and I haven't eaten lunch."

   However, if you have to rack your brain to name anything you like other than your paycheck, it's time to move on.
3. *Are you growing in the job or doing the same things you did when you started?* If you're not growing in a job, what's the point of sticking around? Yes, it's nice to be able to pay your rent and cover your bills, but why settle when you can have both financial security and an exciting job? Six months into a job you should be taking on new responsibilities, projects, and more. In a word, there should be progress. If you're at virtually the same place you started, it may be time to seriously think about whether it's worth staying.
4. *Are your skills marketable?* Everything you do ought to have a dollar value. Naturally, some skills are more marketable than others, yet your job achievements ought to have a clear value. If it turns out you're doing boring work that doesn't translate into transferable skills, it's time to find out what your job prospects are elsewhere.
5. *How far can you go?* When you started, a promotion was promised in a year. But after 6 months with the company, you realize it won't happen for several years. Nobody warned you of the politics that stand in your way. There is the issue of seniority and older workers doing similar jobs who will be considered before you. The boss is not going to throw caution to the wind

and bump you up instead of a senior staffer and risk an age discrimination lawsuit. Put it all together and it's time to package your experience and sell it to another bidder.

6. *Do you like your boss and the people you work with?* I sure hope so. You don't have to be drinking buddies with your boss; mutual respect and appreciation will do. That's about as close to utopia as any employee can expect. And right behind a solid relationship with your boss, it's nice to have the support and friendship of your peers. Some companies are hotbeds of backstabbing politics. Needless to say, it's unpleasant coming to work if this situation exists.
7. *Is management supportive?* Hopefully, your boss is in your corner. But what about senior management? Is it a rigid bureaucracy steeped in a good-old-boys network that rewards friends of management rather than the most capable person? Unless you have a friend or admirer upstairs, no matter how supportive your boss, your future looks bleak.
8. *If you could change anything about your job, what would it be?* If you find yourself compiling a long list, it's time to rethink your situation. But if there are only little things you'd change, stick around. You're foolish to consider moving.
9. *Could you be further along if you worked elsewhere?* If you're plugged into your network, you should know how colleagues in competing firms are faring. Are they advancing faster? Taking on bigger projects? Making more money than you? If so, it's time for soul searching.

If you were brutally honest with yourself, you'll know what course of action to follow. If your tune-up conclusively proves you like your job, stay where you are and continue to do good work. But if it shows discontent, by all means start putting out feelers for a new job. One consideration you probably never thought about is creating your own job. Turn the page and I'll tell you how to do it.

CHAPTER 23

WHO SAID YOU CAN'T CREATE YOUR OWN JOB?

Why wait for someone else to create a job opening? Create your own by uncovering a money-making need and then fashioning a job around it.

It sounds too simple, you say. Maybe it is. But who says everything has to be complicated? Whether you hate your job or you're simply champing at the bit to do something more exciting, no one said you can't create your own job. This job market may be the toughest ever, but it's also the most elastic and creative in terms of opportunities. Because it's so fiercely competitive, employers are more likely to listen to a money-making proposition. Show them how you can boost their bottom lines and I guarantee they'll listen. Uncover a need, tell them how you can meet it, and you've just created your own job. It's being done by astute job searchers all over the country.

Here's what it takes to pull it off.

Research, Research, Research! Big Companies Don't Want to Know You, But Everyone Else Does

Job creation is not for the lazy. In order to create a job you have to know where opportunities can be found. That means conducting an intense investigation. Once you start looking, I guarantee you'll uncover job-creation opportunities all around you. They can be found through information from friends, colleagues, and trade or professional association contacts, or from working with a company in a vendor or sales relationship.

In concept, job creation is simple. A company realizes a pressing need and finds someone to meet it. It's the nature of the need that determines the kind of job that's created. If it's just another body to perform a laborious clerical or physical task, then job creation is a straightforward process. But if a new problem has popped up stemming from expansion, increased workload, or new-product introductions, one or a few people have to be hired. Then, job creation is more complex. It means thoroughly understanding a problem, determining what skills are needed to solve it, the type of person who could best do the job, and finally what dollar value to assign to the job.

It's a pretty logical process. But you'd never know it considering how long it takes large and midsize companies to create a new position. What seems straightforward to you and me turns into a bureaucratic nightmare taking months in many large companies. First, the problem is analyzed and proposals are written, followed by discussions (weeks of meetings), consensus, and finally a solution. A new job has been created.

The more people you have in the decision-making process, the longer it takes. But it's a whole different ballgame in small companies. They can't waste time defining and filling jobs. Once their needs are clear, they speedily find the best person to fulfill them. This is especially true of feisty entrepreneurial companies just out of the starting gate. They're all about surviving and being successful, so they're not about to miss a beat.

This is the type of company you ought to approach with a job creation idea. The smaller, the better. Stay away from large and midsize companies. Most are entrenched in bureaucracy and you'll end up banging your head against a stone wall. Follow this rule of thumb: If the company has a human resources department, stay clear of it.

ADVICE

Try to target companies with fewer than 100 employees. Many aggressively growing small companies are practically screaming for help. Often, this occurs at the critical $5 or $10 million sales mark. At a crucial impasse, these firms need seasoned managers to step in and tell them what to do. Or, on an even smaller scale, a fledgling company launched in an incubator or enterprise zone needs an experienced hand to guide it to the marketplace.

Making Contact
"Hey, Do I Have an Idea for You!"
Write a Killer Proposal

The next step is making contact. You should be pretty good at this by now. You wrote a great selling letter that landed you an interview, then you aced the interview, and now you're comfortably situated in a dead-end job, ready to test new career waters.

Bone up on your writing skills because it's going to take a killer letter to get an appointment to make your pitch.

The proposal ought to describe the following:

1. Insightful understanding of the company and its problems.
2. Why the job is necessary, its components, the skills needed to execute it, and, most important, how the job will translate into revenue either directly or through savings.
3. Reporting relationships. Needless to say, if it's a tiny six-person company, this is not an issue. But if there are 50 or more people in the company, you must explain whom you will

report to and how the new job will be synchronized with the existing company machinery.

Brevity is essential. The proposal should be no longer than one and a half pages.

Now let's write a sample job proposal letter.

June 23, 19XX

Mr. Tommy Toggles
Hot Tubs 'R' Us
234 Lemmonstrasse Blvd.
Cedarneck, OH XXXXX

Dear Mr. Toggles:

I am the senior pool designer at Perky Pools, Inc. in Rapids City, Ohio. Since there aren't many companies in this tiny niche industry, I am well acquainted with your company's prestigious reputation for producing efficient high-quality water environments.

I am in the throes of making a job change and would like to offer my services for your new Hot Tub division. The idea of an expensive, easy-to-assemble hot tub is a brilliant concept. But, the industry scuttlebutt indicates that you're having a difficult time making this division profitable. I know I can help you out.

My industry skills, especially in guiding and supervising newly formed divisions, producing new product lines and setting production schedules, could be very beneficial. What your firm needs, and I hope I'm not being presumptuous, is someone to come in and supervise the entire operation and pull the loose strings together. Whether you call this employee a supervising manager or a chief technician is unimportant. What is important is getting the job done so your division becomes profitable. It's time to see returns.

I'd like to meet with you to explain how I can be of service and what I feel needs to be done.

I've worked in the pool and hot tub industry for 18 years, holding key design and supervisory positions in well known trend-setting companies such as PortaPools, Inc., All-Occasion Pools, and Exotic Pools Ltd.

Within the next 7 days, I will follow up this letter with a phone call so we can set up a mutually convenient appointment.

I look forward to meeting you.

Sincerely,

Guido Bodoni, Jr.

ANALYSIS: How do you rate Guido's letter? I'd give him an A+ for the following reasons: He set up the letter nicely by first stating who he is, so the reader becomes interested. He's not just anyone asking for a job, but a seasoned veteran who knows what he's talking about. Once this is said, he gets right to the meat. By referring to industry scuttlebutt, he makes a point that he's plugged into the industry. He goes right for the bull's-eye by pointing out a problem and offering a solution. Yet he's clever enough not to give too much information. He reveals just enough to whet the reader's appetite so he'll be summoned for an interview. By revealing too much, he'd risk having his ideas stolen before he even got to pitch them. Putting cynicism aside, not everyone plays straight.

Sell Benefits and Tell Me What Has to Be Done

The rest of the process is pretty clear-cut. If your letter hits home, you'll be asked to come in for an interview. Then the pressure is on you to sell your heart out.

Once past the small talk, get right to business. And get ready for serious risk taking. If you got this far, you have no choice but to go all the way in terms of thoroughly explaining the job and why you're the perfect one for it. I know what you're thinking. Who's to say potential employers won't take your great idea and give it to one of their own people? Yes, it's possible. But that's the game you must play. All that can be said is that most people are honest and ethical. *Remember:* Anyone who has gotten anywhere has had the guts to gamble.

When explaining a new job, don't be vague or speak in generalities. Instead, spell out everything in precise detail. *Remember:* This person is hungry for details. From the moment you begin explaining the job, the employer must see benefits, preferably profits. If he or she sees lots of dollar signs, you stand an excellent chance.

There Is No Such Thing as Defeat

Even if you don't hook your interviewer and score, you've captured selling experience, the next best thing to a job. If you can create a job for one company, you can do it for another. Don't get discouraged. Instead, refine your act and take it on the road.

If you do succeed, bear in mind that job creation can be a steppingstone to entrepreneurship.

CHAPTER 24

WHAT? YOU'VE HAD IT PLAYING THE JOB GAME! YOU'RE <u>ACTUALLY</u> THINKING OF STARTING YOUR OWN BUSINESS

Entrepreneurship is not for everyone. Get beyond the romantic notion and find out if you've got what it takes to be a business owner.

Running one's own business is the dream of a lifetime for millions of people. In the wake of nonstop downsizing, many corporate refugees see it as a godsend or a form of salvation. Before we go any further, let's apply the brakes and wave a cautionary red flag: *Entrepreneurship is not for everyone.* What often looks like a dream can turn into a nightmare if you don't know what you're getting into.

Often, job creation is the first step to business ownership. The reasoning goes like this: "If I could create a job, why couldn't I create a business?" It sounds logical, but it's flawed reasoning. While it takes creativity to create a job or a business, that's where the comparison ends. Once you create a job and get someone to hire you, you become an employee. You may be smart and enterprising, but you're an employee nonetheless. Someone is taking care of you and paying you every week like clockwork. Business ownership is something else entirely.

Still, job creation can lead to business ownership if it stokes dormant entrepreneurial fires inside you. But if it's not in you, don't even consider it.

Let's learn more about entrepreneurship.

The Hard Facts of Business Ownership

If you think working for a company is risky, wait till you hear the hard facts about entrepreneurship. From the onset, the odds are stacked against you. According to the U.S. Small Business Administration, three out of five new companies perish within their first 3 years of operation. Yet those forbidding statistics don't discourage anyone from trying. More than 10 years of downsizing have prompted record numbers of entrepreneurs to try their hands at business ownership. It can be likened to the gold rush to the western frontier at the turn of the century. Thousands of uprooted corporate refugees see business ownership as their road not only to wealth, but also to regaining their dignity and self-respect.

Paul D. Reynolds, Coleman Foundation professor of Entrepreneurial Studies at Marquette University in Milwaukee, reports that more people are starting companies each year than are getting married. According to Reynolds, a record 1 in every 25 adult Americans is trying to launch a business. Reynolds estimates that the number of prospective company owners in the United States (approximately 7 million) exceeds the entire population of Massachusetts or Missouri.

But, in this case, there is not strength in numbers. Don't be sidetracked by incredible fantasies of wealth, power, and freedom. Since so many people are starting companies, the entrepreneurial marketplace is more competitive than ever. As for enjoying the good life, most entrepreneurs never get the chance to taste the fruits of their labor. Whether it's a tiny two-person operation barely clearing $100,000 a year or a thriving company employing 20 and hitting sales of $5 million, count on the entrepreneur putting in 10- and 12-hour days, 6 days a week. The rest of the time, they're either thinking or worrying about their business. And for good reason. Any business owner will candidly tell you the first 2 years are the make-or-break years.

Whether entrepreneurs start with $1000 or $1 million, all their energy is focused on succeeding. Their goal is to create a business providing a product or service that has a life all its own. In fact, successful entrepreneurs have compared growing a business to raising a child. Parents never know how a child will turn out, no matter how caring or devoted they are. It's much the same with a new business. If entrepreneurs make prudent decisions combined with good timing and marketing prowess, they stand a chance of seeing their business reach adolescence and succeeding. Yet, as with raising a child, poor decisions and not heeding early warning signs could lead to devastating problems.

One thing is certain: Entrepreneurs give it everything they have. Whereas many established businesses borrow money from banks, family members, or venture capitalists, most entrepreneurs use their own money to get the venture going. Some take out a second mortgage on their homes and still others run up incredible sums on their credit cards to foot start-up costs. Regardless of where the funding comes from, entrepreneurs' identities soon are entwined with those of their businesses.

Losing a job can be devastating. But failing at a business is worse. Beyond the loss of vast sums of money, it's also a shattering blow to the ego. Even if an accident or act of God destroyed everything the entrepreneur worked for, it's still often interpreted as a personal failure. Entrepreneurs are hardest on themselves. They feel they're being judged by family, friends, and even the community at large.

But just don't take my word for it. Do your own research. Read biographies of superstar entrepreneurs, such as Andrew Carnegie,

Cornelius Vanderbilt, Jay Gould, John Davison Rockefeller, and, more recently, R. David Thomas, and a clear picture of the entrepreneurial personality will emerge. The trials and tribulations involved in building their empires is the stuff of miniseries. The story of how Thomas launched Wendy's (*Dave's Way*) is an inspiring tale of suffering, hardship, tenacity, and compulsive devotion. But like every successful entrepreneur, Thomas worked feverishly and encountered setbacks, yet his single-minded obsession wouldn't allow him to consider failure.

Do You Have What It Takes?

Put it all together and it takes a strong, resilient, and confident person to launch a business. A pioneer mindset, a hearty constitution, and a willingness to work around the clock are needed to get your business off the ground. Not everyone is willing to make that commitment. It's no crime if you don't have the constitution for it.

The answers to the following questions will help you decide whether to consider business ownership.

1. *Do you have a high tolerance for risk?* Holding on to a job is a walk in the park compared to business ownership. With business ownership, the odds are stacked against you from the start and you can't be discouraged or depressed about this harsh reality.
2. *Can you handle rejection?* As soon as you ask for help, whether it be in the form of money or advice, you're going to experience some rejection. It may even be from people close to you, such as family and friends. It could sound something like, "Are you nuts? You're actually going to start a business. You have no idea what you're in for. What the heck do you know about running a business? If I were you, I'd look for another job so you can pick up where you left off and take home a weekly paycheck. You're going to be eaten alive." It sounds brutal. But people can be cruel. More difficult is developing a tough skin that allows you to determine what's true, sadistic, or just old-fashioned envy.

3. *Can you take criticism?* As with rejection, be prepared for criticism as well. In fact, smart business owners seek it. The trick is to distinguish between just and unjust criticism. Doing so can be tough. It means taming your ego and not letting your feelings get in the way.
4. *Can you cope with uncertainty and stress?* If you can't, don't even consider entrepreneurship. For 2 to 3 years, you're going to be living and breathing uncertainty 24 hours a day. That means plenty of sleepless nights. Yes, many entrepreneurs are successful from the onset. Whether they had astute planning skills or simply had the good fortune to be in the right place at the right time, they got off to a profitable start. But they're the exception, not the rule. Unfortunately, most owners have to wade through minefields of stress before they become profitable. It goes part and parcel with the entrepreneurial lifestyle.
5. *Do you have organizational skills?* If you don't, I sure hope you can soon afford to hire someone who does. In the beginning, you'll have to be a jack-of-all-trades and a master of them too. You're going to be juggling many balls at once and you'll have to learn how to catch them all. By sheer necessity, today's new business owner is forced to act as a virtual company. It means creating the product, supervising the manufacturing and distribution aspects, and then marketing and selling the item. That translates to being more than a little schizophrenic. Hopefully, it will only be temporary. If you don't self-destruct along the way, you'll get to a point where you can afford to hire a couple of people to help out.
6. *Are you flexible, adaptable, and willing to change?* Once again, your answer ought to be affirmative. Every successful company has had to stop and start on a dime and veer off in a new direction when something wasn't working. Often, this happens without any warning signs. Suddenly, a competitor jumped into the market and stole a big customer or convinced an important vendor not to do business with you. Continuing on the same course could mean sudden death.

7. *Are you persistent?* Entrepreneurs must have the persistence of pit bulls. Without it, the majority would quit just weeks after starting. Most entrepreneurs say that things seldom fall into place as planned. They find themselves coping with more resistance than they ever imagined. Only the tough-skinned, persistent ones make it.
8. *Can you live without the supportive feedback of coworkers?* This may seem like an insignificant detail. But anyone who's spent a considerable time working for others might miss it. Everyone jokes about time spent around the water cooler trading information, sharing war stories, or commiserating with coworkers. It doesn't seem important when you look back on corporate life, but it's something easily missed when you're on your own. Time spent chatting with coworkers amounted to valuable downtime during which you could vent, recharge your batteries, and, most important, share experiences and feelings.

Unless you have an angel guiding the business and acting as a mentor, you're going to be on your own. The proverbial buck stops at your feet. On top of everything else, entrepreneurship can be lonely at times.

It sounds pretty forbidding. But that's only if you're not cut out to be a business owner. If you are hell-bent on trying it, nothing will discourage you—not even walking over hot coals.

Well Okay, So I'll Learn How to Be an Entrepreneur Anyway

What do you do if you didn't do well with the above questions, but still want to give entrepreneurship a shot? For years, business scholars have been debating whether entrepreneurial skills can be acquired. The answer is a tentative "maybe." While no hard evidence exists, I'm almost convinced an entrepreneurial gene exists predetermining many business creators for success. It transcends education and socioeconomic background. Many superstar entrepreneurs who've launched billion-dollar businesses didn't even complete high school. R. David Thomas (Wendy's), Al Copeland (Popeye's), and Richard Branson (Virgin Airways) are three who come to mind. Each man had an innate—and unexplainable—gift for business creation.

Professor William D. Bygrave at Boston's Babson College says you can teach entrepreneurial basics, strategies, and tools of the trade, yet if the natural talent is missing, success won't occur. Other experts contend that successful entrepreneurs have an "entrepreneurial personality," consisting of certain traits all entrepreneurs share. These traits include "streetfighter personality," "self-starter," "highly motivated," "workaholic/compulsive personality," "creative problem solver," and "the ability to turn adversity into a learning experience."

Nevertheless, more than 300 colleges and universities across the United States insist that entrepreneurial skills can be learned. These schools offer an impressive battery of courses and degree programs in all phases of entrepreneurship.

So, what's the solution? If you're itching to take a shot at entrepreneurship, by all means try. But do it smartly. Whether you have that elusive entrepreneurial gene or "natural talent" as Bygrave calls it, take the time to learn everything you can about running a business before you start. Take courses and, by all means, talk to other entrepreneurs. Shower them with questions or, better yet, hang out with them for a couple of days so you can get a glimpse of what the entrepreneurial lifestyle is really like. Then, make your decision. If you decide you're not cut out to be a business owner, you've wasted neither your time nor your money. In fact, you've benefitted because you learned something about yourself.

Now, let's wind down with some thoughts on retirement.

CHAPTER 25

RETIRE? ARE YOU NUTS?

RULE 25 Retirement is a failed concept. You're better off working till you drop.

Why do we make such a big deal about retirement? As we get older, it's understandable to think about changing the way we work. Slowing down, relocating, and testing new career waters are all likely possibilities. Even though we complain about our bosses and difficult customers and vendors, most of us enjoy our work. We even enjoy complaining about it. It's part of the ritual called "work." But retire? Why would anyone stop doing something that gives him or her intense pleasure and challenge?

The simple explanation can be traced to the 40 years of relative security that Americans experienced following World War II. Companies, large and small, used retirement as a combination reward and housecleaning tool to bring in fresh blood. The old codgers were given a gold watch, a pension, maybe a cash gift, and then sent off to spend the rest of their days in comfy retirement playing golf, pruning their gardens, and taking the trips they had put off all their lives.

Compounding the problem, the idyllic notion of retirement is reinforced in TV and print ads by companies peddling retirement homes, time-sharing plans, and affordable travel packages for seniors. Utopian ads show silver-haired prosperous-looking couples decked out in snappy summer attire languishing in the sun and looking as if they stumbled into Valhalla.

So, here we are in the most uncertain job market ever and this unrealistic fantasy of retirement is still being shoved down our throats. Now the truth. First, thanks to rampant downsizing, fewer Americans can afford to retire than in the past. Second, even if they could, most of them would soon be twiddling their thumbs out of sheer boredom. If you don't believe me, ask some retired folks how they have adjusted to a life of interminable vacations. I guarantee the majority were bored by the third month.

Work Till You Drop
You've Got to Have a Reason for Getting Up in the Morning

Why do we keep on hyping retirement? Maybe it's for the same reason that few people question résumés and other established traditions. The answer is we're comfortable with them. They've been around so long, we think they have validity. But, as you're quickly discovering, many of the traditions handed down to us are no longer cutting it. The solution is obvious. If something doesn't work, no matter how long it's been around, abort it and find a better way.

A more practical and healthier concept than retirement is what I call the "work-till-you-drop school of thought." It stems from our innate need to be busy. Most of us thrive on structure, challenge, and excitement. Let's not forget money either. Some of us are financially secure, but most Americans can't afford to retire at 65 and live off their savings, pensions, and investment portfolios. And there's another tired myth most of us have been taught since we were kids. It goes like this: If you work smart, save, and invest prudently, you'll have enough to live on when you retire. Part of that fantasy hinges on being able to live comfortably on social security benefits. Yet, as I said in the Introduction, the sobering reality is social security can no longer meet our retirement needs.

Beyond the important financial considerations, the concept of working till you drop is not just about money. It's also about having a reason to get up in the morning. What better example than the countless multimillionaire entrepreneurs who have sworn they'd never retire after trying retirement for a few months or even for a couple of years. They've tried world cruises, hunted big game in the African wilds, and even taken up daredevil sports like skydiving and auto racing. But after they tried all the things they'd put off all their lives, they quickly became bored. No matter how exciting these things were, it paled in comparison to working 8 hours a day at something they loved. This applies to entrepreneurs of all ages.

In fact, many older entrepreneurs unable to cope with retirement reported wide-ranging physical and psychological ailments ranging from ulcers, heart attacks, and back pain to devastating depression. In some rare cases, premature retirement triggered excessive alcohol and drug use. But as soon as these entrepreneurs went back to work, all symptoms disappeared.

Heed the advice of A. J. Richard, the 87-year-old founder of P. C. Richard & Son, a $500-million-a-year electronics empire. Like clockwork, Richard can be found in his office 5 days a week smoking a Jamaican cigar and sipping strong black coffee. Quitting high school after his sophomore year to build his empire out of a tiny hardware store in New York City, Richard has been working 12-hour days most of his life. Twenty years ago, he could have thrown in the towel and lived in the lap of luxury. He could have indulged himself with homes, boats, planes, cars—you name it. Instead, he prefers to live in a comfortable but modest house and drive himself to and from work every day. He gets anxious when he is away from his company for any length of time. A. J. on retirement: "I'd never retire. If I couldn't work, I'd die."

But lots of people are actually enjoying retirement. They love the freedom of being able to do all the things they couldn't do earlier in their lives. However, they're the exceptions. Most of us are victims of a culture that celebrates work.

Put it all together and the message is loud and clear: Keep on working at something you enjoy. Stop only to reappraise your situation so you get maximum satisfaction. Follow the advice of R. David

Thomas, Wendy's founder and the man credited with putting the hamburger on the map: "I'd never stop working. I can't think of anything else to do that's more fun."

Remember those words every time you think about throwing in the towel.

INDEX

ABOUT THE AUTHOR

Bob Weinstein is a nationally known and respected journalist, author, and trendwatcher in the career field. His work has appeared in such publications as *The New York Times*, *The Boston Globe, Family Circle, McCall's, Reader's Digest, Us, Crain's New York Business, Newsday,* and *Entrepreneur.* Weinstein has written nine other books on careers, including the acclaimed *Résumés Don't Get Jobs, "So What If I'm 50?"* (both published by McGraw-Hill), *"I'll Work for Free," Jobs for the 21st Century,* and *How to Switch Careers*. Bob Weinstein lives in New York City.